Kenneth M. Moffett, AIA

ARCHITECTURE'S NEW STRANGENESS:
A 21ST CENTURY CULT OF PECULIARITY

T0344410

ORO
EDITIONS

ORO Editions
Publishers of Architecture, Art, and Design
Gordon Goff: Publisher

www.oroeditions.com
info@oroeditions.com

Published by ORO Editions

Author: Kenneth M. Moffett, AIA
Book Design: Ahankara Art
Managing Editor: Jake Anderson

10 9 8 7 6 5 4 3 2 1 First Edition

ISBN: 978-1-951541-72-9

Color Separations and Printing: ORO Group Ltd.
Printed in China.

ORO Editions makes a continuous effort to minimize the overall carbon footprint of its publications. As part of this goal, ORO Editions, in association with Global ReLeaf, arranges to plant trees to replace those used in the manufacturing of the paper produced for its books. Global ReLeaf is an international campaign run by American Forests, one of the world's oldest nonprofit conservation organizations. Global ReLeaf is American Forests' education and action program that helps individuals, organizations, agencies, and corporations improve the local and global environment by planting and caring for trees.

FOR ALISON

"There is a danger when every building has to look spectacular; to look like it is changing the world."

— David Chipperfield

TABLE OF CONTENTS

I. MANIFESTATIONS OF PECULIARITY

II. ODD INS AND OUTS

INTRODUCTION

A well-known architect once famously opined, in a moment of exasperation, that 98% of what gets built and designed today is s**t. One has a suspicion that this is closer to the truth than most of us architects would care to admit. Certainly, this country's ordinary streetscape architecture, with occasional exceptions, confronts us with a dismal array that offers precious little grace, respite or wonder. Strip centers, mcmansions, et al are easy targets, the product of a lowest common denominator condition shared among users, clients, developers, bankers, engineers, and architects themselves, notwithstanding a smattering of good individual buildings and attempts at thoughtful urban developments. Those of us with a modicum of awareness know it's bad, from sea to shining sea, and have a pretty good idea why.

But that is not our subject. By and large the mission is to focus not on that vast and depressing expanse but on what we used to call foreground buildings: the attempts to stand out from that background. You know them when you see them, and all common building types may be represented—residential, commercial, institutional, the lot—but the distinguishing characteristic is that of standing out from the pack in some way. In and of itself this is not a bad thing; the most admired buildings from time immemorial to the present have achieved that status by doing something different: not necessarily by being flashy, but through a fresh or refined take on materials, massing, details, proportions, contextual relationships. Now, the appellation of *merde* was meant to apply, one presumes, to the great unwashed of architecture and cityscape, and not necessarily to our foregrounders—at least, not quite so much. But there are issues of accelerating peculiarity in recent times that do apply to many of the latter, and an examination of those *is* our subject.

The broad-brush evolution of architecture through history consists of long periods of development and refinement, interrupted by lacunae such as the "dark ages" or game changers such as the industrial revolution. Moving on, James Stevens Curl brings us exhaustively through the 19th and early 20th century origins of modernism in a recent controversial book, only to heap vitriol on the Le Corbusiers, Mies van der Rohes, and Gropiuses of early modernism itself, and pretty much everything that has happened since. Notwithstanding the deserved status of certain buildings from "modern times" as masterworks, one is inclined to agree that a certain measure of that vitriol is indeed warranted.

But care should be taken to divide and assign it as deserved: architects, yes, but capitalism, education (primarily a lack thereof), and hubris have worked together until the present day to bring us a lot of bad buildings. There's the co-option of modernism by capitalism, with cheap and dull results, and then the endless isms that schools, journalists, scholars, and practitioners came up with as the 20th century marched forth into the 21st. Modernists may disdain the "battle of the styles" of the early 20th—not to mention the huge predominance of "traditional-lite" stylistic construction on up to the present day—but the same arched brow could be directed at a fair amount of the likes of so-called late modernism, rationalism, minimalism, structuralism, post structuralism, postmodernism, deconstructivism, neo-historicism, blobism, neo-formalism, post-colonialism, parametricism—well, sorry if I left out your particular favorite ism. Since rehearsing any of this further is not my goal, may I avoid the battle of terms and just call it all Modernism? Convenient if not very scholarly. But this book is not meant to be a vessel for obscure footnotes or a means to career advancement. I have no direct ties to the academy and need not publish to avoid perishing, and the AIA has no categories for awarding predominantly negative critiques of the work of its own members.

So what is the time frame of this discussion? Stripped classicism, Art Deco, and some European innovations—"transitional-modernist" styles—were influential from the '20s through the '40s, while the '50s and '60s saw the debasement by market forces of the Corbu/Mies/Gropius precedent into a great many dull boxbuildings. Partially in reaction to this, most of the isms noted above proliferated—some briefly—in the '70s, '80s, and '90s. With that microhistory of modernism in the last century, let's say this book is concerned with what has happened since, in the 21st.

. . .

Computers have been a huge boon to architecture practitioners: drafting machines and parallel bars were but incremental improvements over the 19th century's T square and triangle, though it took a while for a screen and mouse to replace those tools. Software evolved more quickly, to the point that irregular, non-Euclidean delineation could be readily produced and then communicated to the builder. I would offer that this also represented something of a Pandora's box having been opened, for along with greatly increased versatility came the need for discernment in application. In short, the combination of factors that led to so many bad buildings in the eras leading up to the onset of the computer in architecture—collectively, an inadequacy of discernment—now had a far wider range of design possibilities to risk applying badly.

The advent of computer aided design as THE tool in the architectural design process, maker machines notwithstanding, is not the only cause of a flowering of some very cool buildings and a greater number of bad ones in the 21st. It has worked hand in glove with that devil, the internet. These digital giants may deserve equal praise and equal blame.

. . .

As the title on the cover indicates, we are concerned with architecture's newly strange and peculiar manifestations. While it may be deemed superficial to judge a book by its cover, it's fair to say that the way buildings present themselves to the world—the form they take in the process of dividing the outside from the inside—is a crucial aspect of their place in the world. An examination of the markedly odd as manifest by some recent architecture reveals an interesting sort of outline of the ways this has been happening. To wit, we find:

- **Obscuration:** Oddity manifest, though shape *unchanged-*

- **Fragmentation**: Shape changed peculiarly, by various means of *breakage-*

- **Deformation**: Shape changed curiously, by various means of *distortion-*

- **Degradation**: Shape changed questionably, by various means of *removal*.

The lion's share of what follows will flesh out specific approaches to each of these "techniques" by resorting to a sort of case study method, casting a critical eye on some pertinent built projects of the present century. So rightly or wrongly, the form's the thing in this set of critiques. That said, what we find by looking around *inside* and *outside* such questionable buildings is also crucial to an examination thereof, and discussions of both will also follow.

As a final note to the fore, one can hardly avoid multiple mentions of a number of so-called starchitects in writing of this sort, so to the Gehrys, Hadids, Ingelses, Koolhaases and the rest, I intend that my effort will be to avoid anything ad hominen and concentrate on fair-enough commentary about the works.

Illustration numbers 1.15, 2.1, 3.8, 3.15, 3.19, 3.24, 3.26, 3.28.1, 4.10.1, 4.18, 4.19.3, 4.21, 4.23 and 4.27 appeared originally in the author's book, *Forming and Centering: Foundational Aspects of Architectural Design*, published by Emerald Publishing in 2017, and are used by permission.

PART ONE

MANIFESTATIONS
OF PECULIARITY

OBSCURATION: ODDITY MANIFEST, YET SHAPE UNCHANGED

This current-century desire to innovate in formative terms has one manifestation which is a bit paradoxical: the form itself is not changed; only the appearance of the surface. This could be considered, depending on the circumstances, either the most timid or the most elegant of the newly odd in architecture. And, also a bit paradoxically, approaches along these lines have gravitated to two opposite extremes: one that adds surficial treatments to make a form appear more substantial, the other to make it appear *less* so.

1a. Variegating: Elaboration at the Surface

In this era of the peculiar, it's often a big budget that permits the excesses that concern us. But far more often, indeed as regards the vast majority of buildings in the 21st, budgets are normal: that is, very modest. In spite of this fact, the urge to express—to signify "creativity"—remains apparent, even when the budget is low and there may actually be nothing particularly appropriate about an elaborated design. Of course, the default building volume among that vast majority is commonly little more than a rectangular solid, and attempts at design enhancement often comprise elaboration that is limited primarily to surface effects thereon.

Precedents

Such a desire to elaborate architectonic surfaces has deep roots in the past. It can sometimes seem almost a "fractal" phenomenon, with each element elaborated and those elements featuring in turn their own elaboration, etc. The sequence from early Romanesque leading to high Gothic represents a steady increase in the elaboration and development of surfaces and volumes. Baroque and rococo designs continued the phenomenon in their own vocabularies. The compulsion to elaborate did not always lead to convincing results: witness the awkward appliques of Rome's Porta Pia or

Pavia's Certosa (Fig. 1.1). It seems plausible to suggest that a weariness with this evident belief of "more is better," up through Gothic revival and beyond, was a major instigator of the onset of modernism.

In turn, ironically, our species' documented need for structure and detail in its environment has given rise to this cheapened elaboration of modernism's cheapened simplification. And in contrast to the dimensional modeling of those precedents, we find that the need to cheapen has flattened it to mere surface or near-surface efforts. A pertinent forebear from the more recent past would be Michael Graves' Portland Building, decorated by pilasters, garlands, and mega-keystones all mere inches in relief, its pairs of tipped-out "sconces" being the only exceptions. (To be sure, this is not all as intended: "value engineering," the architect's curse, shaved off the roofscape elements, projecting belvedere, and three-dimensionally developed garlands, notably flattening the overall work.)

Blank Wall "Enhancement"

Take something as simple as a volume partially clad in a grid of flush metal panels, a reasonable enough material choice for a commercial or institutional application (and certainly a desirable step up from synthetic stucco in most cases). But surely many of us have seen applications where the basic color is mixed in with a range of darker or lighter versions of that color. Sometimes the evident intent is to "patinate" the overall wall appearance—to lend a little variegation to what would otherwise be a large and dull surface: a fair enough goal, when a budget lacks the natural patination qualities of sheet copper, for example. Apparently, though, to judge from the results one sees, this is hard to achieve with a manufacturer's standard range of colors (or may simply be hard for some designers to achieve, period, regardless of the colors available), and the result is a jarringly overscaled pixelization.

1.1 Certosa di Pavia, Lombardy, Italy

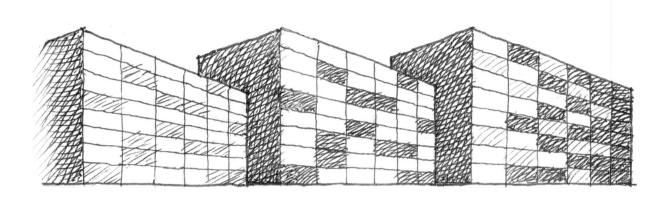

1.2 Metal Panel Variants: "Patinated;" Contrasting; Gradated

This sometimes giving the unintended and certainly undesirable impression that damaged panels have been replaced and that the original color is longer matchable.

Often, though, the pixelization is clearly intentional, featuring substantial degrees of contrast. The approach may be monochrome or (heavens) multi-color, or may feature a dark to light gradation across the façade (Fig. 1.2). I've been trying manfully to give these efforts a chance; to achieve some understanding of the benefits of this tactic. But the approach just ends up looking like a cheap trick: often gaudy, a misbegotten attempt to be "artful" with the coarsely scaled medium of large metal panels. It basically subverts the whole idea of the medium, really, being one of achieving a sleek surface interrupted only by its thin grid of joints. Maybe it's an understandable thing to try when unavoidable constraints lead to a large blank wall, but it ends up contrasting and competing with other exterior elements of the architecture, and not in a good way.

A different but related technique to "elaborate" such a wall has cropped up involving a pattern of low relief, with individual rectangular panels set slightly proud of the main wall surface (Fig. 1.3). They may form some sort of repeating pattern, or may be randomly located, but the undesirable result is largely the same: while it's apparent that the effect is deliberate, an unintended sense of "poor craft" emerges. The low relief, made possible by panels in a variety of thicknesses offered by some suppliers, can end up offering a self-defeating impression that these panels were supposed to be flush but have popped out a bit for some unfortunate reason—

In a sort of ultimate pulling-out-of-the stops in this game of feeling obliged to "variegate" a panelized façade, variously colored panels in varying *depths* have been combined with panels of varying *widths*, stacked up into "strata" distantly reminiscent of coursed ashlar in masonry. The good news is that this richer mix of interacting variables can result in a convincing design, but the bad news is that this requires a very subtle touch and that the more likely result is an exercise in wholly unnecessary busyness. Ultimately, in reviewing the downsides of these not uncommon "enhancements," it occurs that there's really *nothing wrong* with an unarticulated, mono-colored wall of flush metal panels, the ever-present proviso being that it is part and parcel of a well-considered overall composition.

13

If the goal of these efforts is, in effect, to "decorate" an otherwise largely blank panelized façade, Herzog & de Meuron took that goal to another level at their library in Eberswalde, Germany, where enlarged images from photographs and paintings were applied by screen printing techniques onto gridded bands of concrete and glass. One interesting effect was the "blending" of the glazed bands with the concrete bands, such that there isn't much in the way of any intermediate scale development between the extremes of the overall volume and this applied pictorial patterning, aside from some unartful punched openings (Fig. 1.4). As a result, there is an odd juxtaposition of this fine-grained and repeating monochromatic detail with the direct mundanity of the box building, as if to distract from or dematerialize it, and in this regard the project constitutes a sort of link between this discussion of variegation and the next of dematerialization.

Wall Opening Pattern Variegation

This compulsion to add variety to a large and plain wall surface has manifesting itself in some other ways in the last couple of decades. When the façade is fenestrated, we note that the vicissitudes of style preference have evolved, as evolve they will, since the early days of modernism. Once "ribbon windows" became buildable, if not especially economical, we saw their well-known appearance in iconic buildings such as the Villa Savoye, and before long the continuous ribbon window became an accepted and ubiquitous treatment for commercial architecture, recurring to this day. (The advent of the curtain wall saw the proliferation of the even more ubiquitous glass screen—the entirety

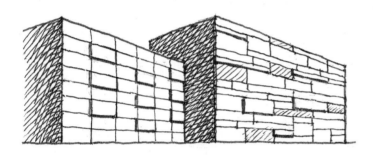

1.3 Metal Panel Variants: Proud Panels; Mixed Widths/Lengths/Depths /Colors

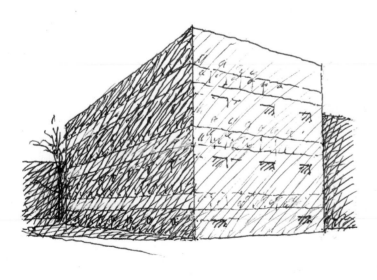

1.4 Eberswalde Technical School Library, Eberswalde, Germany

of the wall itself having become glass—but that is a different animal that doesn't directly pertain to this particular issue.)

In the '70's, a grid pattern of square "punched" windows in masonry (or in EIFS, the material that wants to be plaster that wants to be masonry) became the rage for a time (Fig. 1.5.1). A well-respected colleague, a fan of the ribbon, once complained about the illogic of a punched approach, in defying Corbu's advocacy of the ribbon's even lighting and breadth of outlook, but logic plays only a limited part in such design choices, both then and now. Of course, the true precedent for this approach was the masonry bearing wall of the past wherein punched openings, their widths limited by a lintel's load-bearing capacity, was the norm. In any case, nowadays such changes are generally due simply to an accumulating boredom with what was once popular, leading to a new latest-and-greatest, and, often enough, back again.

(Some examples of interior finishes exemplify this circularity especially well: walnut-birch-walnut; brass-silver-brass; green-anything else-green; etc.)

It's interesting how this sequence leads, in turn, to the more recent popularity of narrow *vertical* punched-opening windows. (Dare we call it a prison-bar effect?) Such vertical "slots" may vary in width and in spacing, sometimes arbitrarily with respect to conditions on the interior. Or if these idiosyncratic spacings do faithfully reflect different room widths or whatever, when walls move in the future to accommodate new needs or tenants the correspondence is likely to become, well, peculiar. True, this variegated vertical array approach has been carried out well in some handsome buildings, but it is all those others that concern us here. These slot window widths and spacings vary from floor to floor as well, spacing-wise, and an appropriately scaled edge

1.5.1 Window Pattern Variants: Ribbons; Punches; Slots
1.5.2 Variants on the Variants: Eroded Ribbons, Punches & Slots

band is important to avoid a sense that the game of jenga is about to go south, with openings slipped halfway off the one below and the like. And yet sometimes the floor lines go away altogether in questionable morphing about with these slots, not to mention punches and ribbons as well (Fig. 1.5.2).

. . .

In this apparent ongoing project to treat repeating window openings in a way that distracts attention from their very repetitiousness, some further variations on the theme have been essayed (Fig. 1.6):

- **Alternating** vertical and horizontal window proportions, side to side *and* top to bottom: Not every space program would lend itself well to this treatment, and the somewhat disturbing near chaos that results renders the approach a very acquired taste.

- **Connecting** windows vertically with spandrel material *and* alternating the treatment for a staggered effect: staggering indeed, and not in a good way. Possibly effective in an isolated condition, the motif is grimly peculiar when repeated.

- **Slanting** one or both jambs of the window opening, and in a non-repeating array, side

to side and top to bottom. Steven Holl's Glassell School of Art in Houston does so, but along with occasional canted recesses, a speckling of attendant small square operable sash (actually a good thing, both environmentally and compositionally), plus one wing's idiosyncratic, seemingly arbitrary sloped profile. Each such motif in turn would have been just about enough, but the overall impact would seem to be too much of several good things.

Sometimes simplest is best in an effort to vary a repetitive and/or inadequately scaled window pattern. A repeating array of narrow vertical windows can be given surprisingly effective faux variety by alternatingly flanking them with accent panels that, while making no attempt to look like more window, both expand their impact and vary their pattern. An analogous treatment serves a similar role for the regular array of small rectangular windows that often appear as the economical default, by applying a substantial elbow of accent material to each.

Wall Appliqué

A third and larger-scale approach to such variegating comprises "low-relief layering," being a ubiquitous attempt to conceal the flat, boxy nature of midrise developer buildings.

1.6 Window Pattern Variants: Connecting; Alternating; Slanting

1.7 Wall Appliqué: The Sheridan Apartments, Birmingham, Michigan

Such buildings have become common in part as a result of codes permitting a stick-built upper stories above a concrete base structure, resulting in an unfortunate increase in the scale of their boxiness. The simplest version of this approach consists in little more than changing the color of the wall panel system, a variant on the first category above, to add fat two-dimensional "frames" around groups of window openings. In the spirit of varying the façade, these are often made to jump up and down, recalling the "staggered effect" described above; or to vary the number of bays so "enframed;" or to vary the color of the enframing panels. They may simply be flush or feature very shallow relief. The effect is, generally, a very direct communication of what has been done, the façade thus "decorated" doing the facts of its flatness and repetitiveness no favors, but instead generally coming off as amateurishly random and lacking evidence of compositional intentionality.

The budget and building type permitting, such "enframing devices" project a bit from the default façade, either to give the impression of a thick appliqued layer of solid "plane" or, alternatively, a through-passing "collided" element (Fig. 1.7). Often enough, a favored feature of the former is to project the applied plane up from the default parapet, the apparent intention being to vary an otherwise continuous straight roofline, but with the unfortunate result of making the thin and cardboardish nature of the applique even more evident. Variations in material color and/or in fenestration type are further devices in this version's bag of tricks, particularly favored in the case of hotels, the incorrect supposition being that there is something intrinsically bad about letting the fenestration pattern have the dignity of being allowed to repeat for a while.

Another version of applique combines the perceived need to variegate a blank surface with the growing and often ill-advised use of the fashionably angled edge. Whole angled *buildings* are addressed elsewhere; here we see the trend where it appears among more modest low-relief applications. In an apropos example, at Louisville's Southwest Regional Library the sloped parapets of its solid volumes were evidently not considered progressive enough, as those walls are clad in turn with closely overlapped metal-clad planes at intersecting angles (Fig. 1.8). Gilding the lily? They do lend a raffishly chaotic quality: one such angle, referencing the parapet, might have been an appropriate enhancement, but the end result seems a step or two too far.

And speaking of going too far, Zaha Hadid's Broad Art Museum at Michigan State University, which happens to be one of those whole angled buildings, offers a more spectacular and baffling use of contrasting tilts along a façade,

their aggressively "pleated" surfaces offered up as if the building itself, already tilting, needed even more, well, aggressiveness (Fig. 1.9). That treatment does constitute something of an exception to the foregoing, due both to its badass demeanor and the shallow but significant three-dimensional modeling of its facades. The design of most of the buildings in this initial chapter would not be thus characterized as "aggressive": they're here because all the effort, such as it is, is about the surface. Shortly though, bigger, odder things, aggressive things involving breaking, stretching, tipping, twisting and more will take the stage.

1.8 Louisville Free Public Library, Southwest Regional Branch

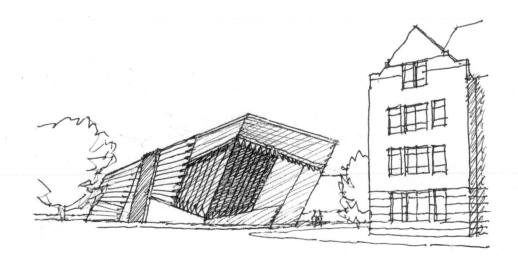

1.9 Eli and Edythe Broad Art Museum, Michigan State University, East Lansing

1b. Dematerializing:
Obfuscation at the Surface

As opposed to variegating, which deals with methods to elaborate a particular volume without materially changing its physical boundaries, another approach could be said to employ opposite methodologies, being reductive rather that elaborative. Instead of adding patterns or low-relief layers, an assortment of means now seeks to make a building go away: to disappear. Well, not really, but the morphological intent is there; one of staying more or less within the bounds of the originating volume but to render it immaterial to a degree; to deny the existence of its faces, edges, and corners, even though they remain.

Take Away the Frame

A ubiquitous and rudimentary version of this approach has been around for decades in the form of buildings wrapped in reflective glass curtainwall, but in the current century, advances in technology (super-reflective glass coatings; mirror-finished aluminum or stainless steel panels; cladding systems with hairline joints) can truly permit a building to be surrealistically in denial. In as perfect a mirror as can be managed, one sees not the building but what the building sees. For one big example, Maraya Concert Hall in the picturesque wastes of Saudi Arabia is clad all but seamlessly with mirror finished opaque glass, achieving this peculiar goal (Fig. 1.10).

A complete reversal of the above intent would render a building completely transparent, such that it denies its presence not by reflecting its context, but by embracing it—by allowing it, in a sense, to continue through without interruption. The famous "glass houses"—the Farnsworth, the Johnson house—did attempt a visual continuity through their glazed perimeters, but more recent technologies have again permitted a more complete, if correspondingly less practical, realization. A well-known example would be the Manhattan Apple Store, or

1.10 Maraya Concert Hall, Al-Ula, Saudi Arabia

rather the glass vitrine entrance leading to the underground store itself (Fig. 1.11). Despite the elegantly minimal detailing, reality imposes a bit of a compromised effect in the form of reflections and other natural effects of light, refraction and air pollution. And the approach, solely on its own terms, deals more with a special effect than functioning architecture.

Lost in the Mist

To move on from the ultimate unrealizability of the above to a simpler one of *blending in*, this can consist of matching the color of the sky with the color of a fritted wrapper. The sky has a way of changing, so it's inevitably a compromise (if in such a case it was ever ultimately a goal to really sort of disappear). Holl's Reid Building of the Glasgow School of Art understates its massiveness in, presumably, deference to the doubly ruined Mackintosh building opposite, being largely clad in sandblasted gray-blue-green spandrel glass (Fig. 1.12).

A clear glass wrapper with applied patterns, images, or frits would be the step up from such "blending into the background." While we've seen silk-screened images on the German library's bands of glazing, the next step would be a fully glazed building volume with an applied pattern. This was done at the John Lewis department store in Leicester by Foreign Office Architects, which involves a complex vine-like pattern of frit applied to inner and outer layers of clear glazing (Fig. 1.13). The silicone seams are minimized, and the outer frit is reflective, the whole indeed adding up from a distance to a sort of mist, albeit one with well-defined edges. The top edge is hardly perceptible when sky conditions are right. The building being a functioning department store as

1.11 Apple Fifth Avenue, NYC

1.12 Seona Reid Building, Glasgow School of Art

1.13 John Lewis & Partners Department Store, Leicester, UK: Doubled Frit Pattern

20

opposed to a minimally functioning vitrine, the doubled glazing in conjunction with the fritted pattern provides a measure of solar control and insulation, while exemplifying a measure of visual dematerialization.

Employing an unfigured frit, as opposed to a patterned one, could be roughly equivalent in effect to Holl's sandblasted glass, but its capacity to be gradated from clear to opaque offers a unique versatility. Gehry's IAC building in Manhattan steps outside the bounds of the sequence of comparisons in this chapter, in that part of its own strategy of dematerialization is to replace all straight vertical edges with edges curving in three dimensions, said to evoke sails, and appearing more evanescent and (from some vantage points at least) weightless as a result (Fig. 1.14). And the frit employed, graded to clear at the eye level at each floor, contributes its foggy quality to the overall effect. I can't resist adding that my first impression of this gradated frit was not an especially flattering one, seeming almost as if the whole building had been sprayed with window cleaner and the clear bands wiped off first so people could see out. All in all, something of an exception in the Gehry oeuvre: getting a bit lost in the mist as opposed to getting in your face.

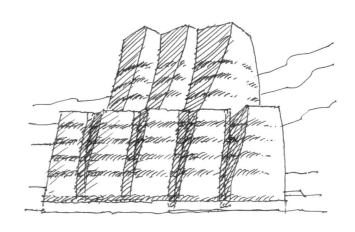

1.14 IAC Building, NYC

A discussion of buildings dissolving into mist would be incomplete without a mention of Diller Scofidio + Renfro's Blur Building, a temporary pavilion for a 2002 Swiss expo at the base of Lake Neuchâtel. Instead of seeking to disappear via total transparency like the Apple pavilion, it disappeared in a cloud (Fig. 1.15). In effect it *was* the cloud, the structure being an open tensegrity strutwork affording no enclosure. The experience was one of the media involved, including the fog, not one of conventionally defined space. As there was no building to attempt to dematerialize in the first place, the project was more novel than pertinent here.

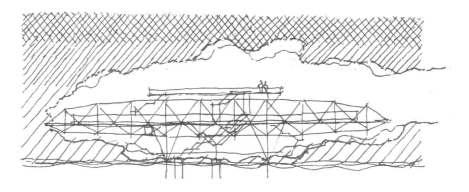

1.15 Blur Building, Yverdon-les-Bains, Switzerland [Demolished]

Delamination

The term doesn't seem quite right, but it sort-of suggests another approach to "dematerializing" an architectural volume. A building as a stack of pancakes, with floor lines clearly expressed, is a commonplace, and a vertical emphasis of linear figuration (such as at Rockefeller Center, for example) could also be considered a common expressive motif. But the point for this discussion is a design that works toward visually removing the three-dimensional nature of a building. It would be, so to speak, partially dematerialized, the result being a ghost defined by arrays of two-dimensional elements. Rows of vertical ribs, depending on the angle of view, exemplify this approach at Lisbon's EDP Headquarters for Portugal's main electrical company, by Aires Mateus, although it's more of a gimmick than a true example in the spirit of dematerialization (Fig. 1.16). True, an effort was made to subsume the buildings' nature as volumes with the device of inexorably marching parallel planes. The way they bypass large elevated open porches as well as extending beyond the parapets to wrap diagonally across the top contribute to a sense of progressive immateriality, and the slowly raising soffit across the street exposure has its own part to play in a contributory sense of weightlessness. In the last analysis, the whole complex of two towers and low-rise link has the elaborately and deliberately crafted look of having been run through a slicer-dicer, but one that removes everything but thin planes: delamination, indeed.

Chicago's Aqua Tower by Studio Gang develops a somewhat analogous idea but with horizontal rather than vertical "laminae" (Fig. 1.17). Again, the rectangular solid of the building is obscured by a series of planes, here artfully wavy to approximate large convexities and concavities: a vaguely pillowy vertical topography complete with so-called "ponds" defining where the slab edges return to meet the curtain wall. The waviness contributes to a bit of a misty quality, as if just beginning to expand outward and diffuse away to nothing. In that regard the "initiating solid" isn't developed at its surfaces but is something of an exception here, exfoliating a bit to achieve this trembly looking outboard treatment. To be honest, the effect can be a bit creepy: I'm not sure why.

Devolution

One more strategy to distance a building from its reality is to present it as a return to the natural world: the enclosure remaining but reimagined, three dimensions devolved to one in terms of the visual remnants. Toyo Ito's Tokyo store for Tod's clads the rectilinear volume with linear criss-crossing concrete diagonals, abstract trees meant to evoke actual trees nearby (Fig. 1.18).

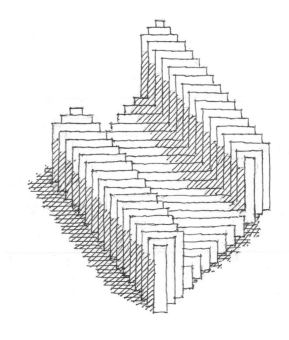

1.16 EDP Headquarters, Lisbon: Axonometric Interpretation of Concept

The building's rectilinear form still has a strong presence—there has been no effort made to hide it in the clouds—but the tree branch imagery suggests a degenerated sort of reality.

The Beijing National Stadium (Herzog & de Meuron with Ai Weiwei) is unofficially known as the Bird's Nest, its seemingly random thatch of linear elements evoking that form of natural imagery (Fig. 1.19). But the stadium's "linear" elements become massive steel boxes at close range, their criss-crossings dramatic yet somewhat wince-inducing. And expensive, especially considering the venue has had no particular ongoing purpose since its initial use during the 2008 Summer Olympics. The point in both cases, from the standpoint of dematerialization as an approach in the service of peculiarity, is the conceit that the building is gone, leaving nothing but a tangle of lines.

· · ·

These several "dematerialized" projects have their pros and cons—indeed, some turn out to be pretty interesting and defensible as architecture, or at least, perhaps, as elegant experiments. They have a place here in that the type is "peculiar" by definition: designing a building to disappear, to one degree or another. Other morphologies will offer essays into markedly less defensible extremes of the odd.

1.17 Aqua at Lakeshore East Apartments, Chicago

1.18 Tod's Omotesando Building, Tokyo

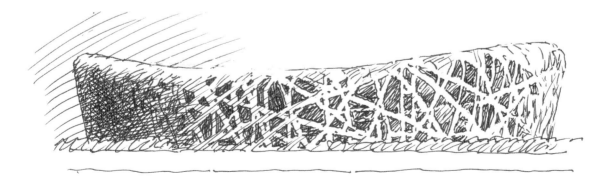

1.19 Beijing National Stadium

23

FRAGMENTATION: SHAPE CHANGED BY BREAKAGE

Say we think in terms of an "initiating form": not necessarily a box building, but something identifiable as a single entity of a building. That was largely the case in the previous chapter where changes were nominally two-dimensional in nature. But now ways are going to appear that modify such a form. The most familiar, it's probably safe to say, consists of variations—three in this discussion—on a theme of breaking things. But the pieces remain, and the form becomes an agglomeration of forms. The approach is a familiar and (sometimes) legitimate one, but nowadays it's being taken to some disturbing extremes.

2a. Stratifying: Disengagement by Layers

Buildings with more than one floor are "stratified" by nature: they're layer cakes, an attribute more intrinsic than any other. So in the urge to do something a little different, a little *odd,* it's natural that playing with these layers will have readily become a thing, in particular since they're there anyway: a messing-around of first resort, with no immediate need to ramp up to major surgery or earthquake-like effects.

Precedents

Italian Gothic comes to mind, its light and dark striping a common result of infilling with cheaper materials, bonding structurally at alternate bands, or trying to exaggerate a building's width. Ultimately in such cases aesthetic impact becomes a means to its own end, adding contrast and pattern to what might be an otherwise plain wall surface. In modern times accent bands in masonry walls have also been popular, but with results often more on the awkward than the elegant side. To wit, James Stirling's No.1 Poultry in London, far from Big Jim's best work, demonstrates that to apply the Italian precedent in equal bands is to misjudge the motif: history's foremost exemplar, Siena Cathedral, reserved the eye-popping equal-zebra-stripe proportions for only select aspects of its fabric.

In Compression

Such enhanced expression of horizontal striation varies widely in scale in pertinent works of the present century, from such wall-pattern figuration to all-out floor-by-floor articulation. Zaha Hadid's Center for Contemporary Art in Cincinnati takes the latter approach, with a predominating impression of its several floors as blocks or bars that have been compressed or collided vertically (though to be sure there are places where the opposite impression prevails, with glass infill between solid masses as if they were separated in *tension*) (Fig. 2.1). Modest lateral shifts as well as contrasting materials are the expressive means. In this early built work of the architect, the constraints of its predominantly solid-walled program plus a limiting urban site have been met, by these ingenious means, to defuse a potentially blocky and massive result. (All well and good, though this may be the first and last opportunity on these pages to praise the architect's contextual sensitivity on an urban site. We shall see.)

Snøhetta's San Francisco Museum of Modern Art Expansion also evokes compression, its big bowed, notched, and carved north face rippled as if a carpet rucked into wrinkles (Fig. 2.2). Its sense of sleekness and continuity doesn't marry that well with the sometimes difficult reality that buildings often need windows, and here they constitute occasionally rude interruptions in that subtly varied continuity. The utter difference of the building from the original Mario Botta museum, of which it is an expansion, has been noted by critics with some measure of displeasure—but it's fair to say that if the museum had wanted more of the same, Botta would have been the logical hire, while Snøhetta will have been far more likely to do something very different, which they did. Botta's building is itself another modern-day interpretation (as are many by the architect) of Florentinish striping at a lavish scale. Ultimately, the two stratigraphic motifs are so completely different that there is no sense of filial connection between them: the addition seems some other project entirely that just happens to be shoved up against the original.

In Tension

Stratifying as a dominating morphology can also evoke the opposite of compression, and in fact a sense of tension or pulling apart is the more ubiquitous among recent exemplars. Mention has been made of "ribbon windows," a type of building striping that alternates continuous bands of glazing with continuous bands of a solid spandrel material:

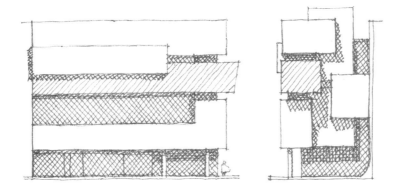

2.1 Contemporary Arts Center, Cincinnati, OH

25

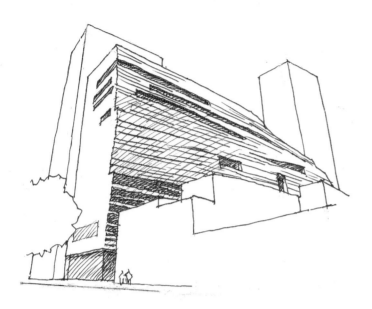

2.2 San Francisco Museum of Modern Art Expansion

2.3 Edmonton International Airport Offices and Control Tower, Alberta, Canada

a volume pulled apart into layers of solid and void. Its original default version finds the glazing continuous for simplicity and internal flexibility, and the spandrel with its raised sill continuous because full height glazing was a cost problem, a heat gain problem, a furnishing problem, and sometimes a privacy problem. In our brave new world these constraints have evolved in a number of ways, but when banded glazing is in the offing nowadays for whatever reasons, the spandrel has tended to metastasize, rising to the challenge of, well, looking like something that isn't a spandrel: preferably, something unusual, and thereby, often, something peculiar.

Edmonton International Airport's office and control tower building, by DIALOG, takes its innocent little spandrels and gives them a constantly varying wiggleworm profile, fatter and thinner, shorter and taller. A subtle sense of axial tension pulls the malleable layers apart, though that could also be attributed to a wind-induced flutter (Fig. 2.3). To its credit some of these variegations respond to practical considerations such as solar and view control, and the effort to transcend the repetitiveness of banding is well-intentioned. Although if looked at in a certain literal-minded way the treatment is clumsy—the spandrels evoking a beginner's pottery handbuilding exercise—the carefully achieved execution affords a sort of self-validation. In fact, many cases of the recently peculiar depend on good materials and execution to help render an oddity convincing: it looks so *real*, so accurate: it must be ok.

While the airport spandrels vary smoothly and within fairly narrow bounds, Hadid's City Life Apartments in Milan carve and stretch the spandrels up and down (and also in and out to a degree). The point for the narrative is the vaguely ripped apart quality of the spandrels, a slightly violent vibe (Fig. 2.4). A sort of ultimate version of this quality appears at Columbia Medical School in Diller Scofido + Renfro's Roy and Diana Vagelos Education Center. The pertinent narrow end of this tallish building stacks up all the interestingly shaped spandrels and slab edges it can find, along with some boxy mix-ins (Fig. 2.5). The diagonals in particular, expressive of sloped seating profiles, emphasize an elastic quality, as if all these pieces once fit together somehow but the thing has been stretched up, the resulting oddly shaped interstices infilled with glass. A number of spandrel faces and other solid elements feature sharply converging diagonals, pushing the ensemble beyond the daring and ingenious into the arguably awkward. There's a sense that maybe those were supposed to line up; that some alignment error crept from drawings into reality. Ultimately this building pushes the subject of spandrel bands past the point where that's not what they really are anymore, so it's a sort of end pin for this sequence of ways to stratifyingly skin a cat (or a building).

. . .

Clearly there is more going on in terms of the form definition of these buildings than varying the shapes of their spandrels: they are all at pains to distance themselves from what a building often wants to be, like it or not, in strictly economic and functional terms: a box. The Cincinnati and Columbia projects articulate their narrower end elevations toward that end, while the Milan project sweeps its corners in a further effort at deboxification. The San Francisco museum addition tortures the long side of its box toward that same goal. It falls to the Edmonton project to be truly something else, with a footprint that is significantly curved, and thereby it has one foot in a later chapter.

2.4 CityLife Apartments, Milan

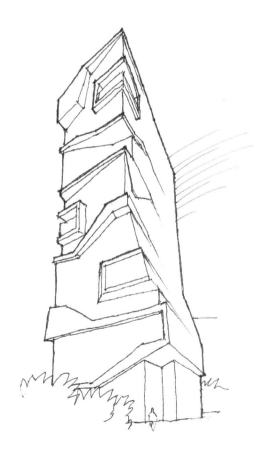

2.5 Roy and Diana Vagelos Education Center, NYC

27

2b. Complicating: One into Many

While **variegating** dealt with taking a simple volumetric development and doing one thing or another at or near its surfaces, with the often misguided goal of adding "interest," **complicating** refers to a larger-scale and more three-dimensional realization of this compulsion. These are both subject to the time-honored problem of not knowing when enough is enough. It's fair to say that a single boxy piece of architecture is, in many cases, likely to be a dull piece of architecture, worthy of some measure of formative development. But the present fallacy sees its opening opportunity when the box is recast as a collection of (or a breaking-apart into) some pieces and parts. And not knowing when to quit has the result of a harmonious composition of architectonic elements becoming, well, disharmonious, whether by dint of too *disparate* an assembly of parts, or of an awkward *disjunction of similar* parts. In either case, consequences of unease, disorientation or sheer sensory overload are the issues that concern us.

Illusion of Multiplicity

There is a sort of gently bogus version of this path to the peculiar which takes a simple, basic form (not necessarily a boxy one) and adds niches, notches, bays, scrims, screens—efforts in the direction of multiple parts, that camouflage that basic form within the elaborations. Among any number of examples of this type, Google finds me a recent addition to the reasonably handsome campus of the Minneapolis Veteran's Home, where a ponderous traditional-lite vocabulary clads a recent building of many apparently collided parts (Fig. 2.6.1). These actually comprise the elaboration of a single

basic volume. While not badly conceived as best one can tell from a cursory view, it seems right to characterize it as having simply gotten a bit too jumped up and overwrought.

In a more modernist mode, one comes across EwingCole's Unisphere: not the spherical theme structure one might vaguely recall, but an admirably net-zero addition to United Therapeutic's biotech campus in Maryland (Fig. 2.6.2). Parts of the exterior are artful enough, but a multiplicity of treatments—metal clad boxes, arced and tilted curtain wall, arced metal mesh scrims, a façade of ranked solar collector eaves,

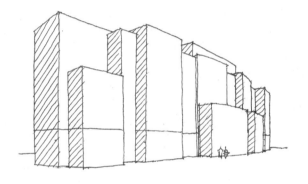

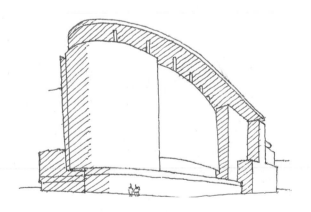

2.6.1 Minneapolis Veterans Home Building 22 (Basic Massing)
2.6.2 Unisphere Building, Silver Spring, Maryland (Basic Massing)

a floating roof plane—again add up to a bit much of a good thing. A compact bullet-shaped volume can be readily visualized as the "originator" from which all this interesting flotsam exfoliated—and in fact this is the very shape of the topmost lid.

Relatively small adjustments can make a big difference in such cases, between pleasurable articulation and fussy multiplicity. Though the contents of the two preceding projects are wholly different, their corresponding images make for an interesting comparison: similarly scaled works, both dealing with illusions of multiplicity, but dressed in the ever-dueling attires of quasi-historicism and modernism.

Disjunction into (or Confluence of?) Disparate Elements

Often, large buildings attract this strategy, the perceived need being to break down and elaborate big walls and volumes. (The familiar *breaking-apart* approach of composing a project as separated building elements, a sort of village compound, in illusion or in reality, doesn't quite belong in the present discussion.)

One means of said complicating is sometimes a two-step process. Similar elements are first aggregated into ensembles-- each ensemble different in character from whatever others there may be--and then these dissimilar ensembles are themselves aggregated (i.e., pushed together). Randall Stout's Art Gallery of Alberta perfectly exemplifies this: a solid-looking and corners-intensive mass of collided rectilinear volumes— the main body of the museum—is enfronted and overreached by a composition of very wavy and curly planar elements (Fig. 2.7). A third set of elements comprising gridded glazed planes

provides enclosure. These variously tipped and tilted planes, in conjunction with the wavy things, inevitably give an unsettling sense that said pieces and parts are barely holding it together: caught in the act of falling down, or perhaps blowing away, or both. This idea of adding a measure of complexity by contrasting differing elements—flat and solid, curly and thin, tilting and transparent—is a bold and promising one in the service of making a place for art exciting, but it is arguably taken several measures too far in this somewhat alarming looking case.

The following may be Gehry Partners' first mention in these pages; it will not be the last. And this should be counted in some ways a compliment, the range of that firm's work being so wide in its formative innovation and sheer risk-taking. Take MIT's Stata Center, as so many others have done once it was completed in 2004 and in the years since. It is nearly unavoidable to join in, the project being a virtual poster child for the morphology of complication (Fig. 2.8).

2.7 Art Gallery of Alberta, Edmonton, Canada

2.8 Ray and Maria Stata Center, MIT, Cambridge, MA

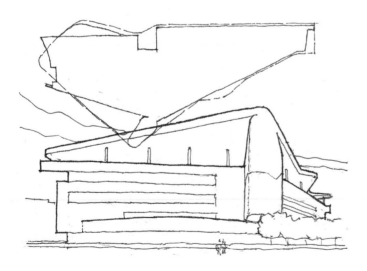

2.9 Emma and Georgina Bloomberg Center, Cornell Tech, NYC

The edifice is truly one of those cases where a very large building calls out for articulation of some sort, and indeed the grimness of adjoining Vassar Street and MIT buildings deeply needed a bolder and more varied centerpiece. That this mission could be said to have lacked the presence of a philosopher king to say hold it, that's about enough, is eminently clear.

We again see a multi-stage process, but different in nature from that in Alberta. Dramatically differing elements do appear, cheek by jowl, in a rough alternation of squared-off brick towers and variously pleated or cylindroid metal towers. But the overall project seems subject to an almost fractalish scaling sequence. Camouflaged by the riot of forms, the project at its most elemental level is actually two tower buildings, which define a plinth/plaza facing the campus. The next scalar level sees the towers masquerading as a *bunch* of towers, variegated as noted. The next level yet sees pleated gadgets (appropriately functional though perhaps overly cartoonish entry canopies) on the street side, and on the campus side an assortment of wild 'n wooly chess pieces milling about on the plinth. Finally, there are the signature Gehry windows, laborious box-extrusions in varying locations on the metal towerettes. It's all actually great fun if you're there for a quick visit and aren't too stuck up about it, but reports of usability, expandability, and durability issues are a less jolly matter. Sticking to the point, though, and it will be difficult to find enough different ways to say this over and over in narratives to follow, it's all too much of a complicated good thing.

Morphosis' Bloomberg Center at the NYC Cornell Tech campus may well be an exemplar of "complication done pretty well" (Fig. 2.9).

The limitations of the site define a potentially awkward scalene triangle of a footprint, but its primary wall planes are disconnected, and the resulting "gaps" developed as specialized features. A floating roof plane for solar collectors finds its own freeform profile to put a lid on the composition, literally and figuratively. Depending on one's vantage point, the prominent stair tower is an arguably false step: it convincingly anchors the roof plane as seen from a distance, but makes some difficult formative conditions at that juncture, implying an uncomfortable "stretch" of the roof plane at this one point where it is contiguously "attached." That said, while the project seems at first glance to exemplify complication with its diverse formative conditions, its vocabulary of elements turns out to be a relatively simple one: complication taken only as far as warranted.

Confluence of (or Disjunction into?) Similar Elements

While the above basically addresses horizontally massed buildings, with their elements brought together as ensembles, a different means of complication arises with buildings of some height. A few stories suffice, but towers seem to be particularly attracted to this little game, namely "cracking" the volume at one or more points and imposing a twist or a shove or both in each case. And true, it's equally plausible to visualize this as an additive process, with individual elements stacked up in a jenga pile. While "stratifying" dealt with the over-elaboration of a taller building's nature as a stack of floors, here the issue is more abstract. Manhattan's New Museum by SANAA is a fairly well-mannered

case, its stacked boxes remaining orthogonal to each other, eschewing dramatic overhangs, and subtly reducing in scale on ascent. But as in so many creative pursuits, there is a point in the use of this approach where things get a bit out of hand. Godefroy Tang's "Opera Cube Tower" in Foshan, China, while also maintaining orthogonal relationships, manages to achieve a very uneasy sense of instability with its maximized overhangs, apparently for that reason only (Fig. 2.10). While the Big Brothers of China have been asking for less in the way of deliberately weird architecture, perhaps rightly fearing the industrialized world may think them a bit out of control on their way to world dominance, it's clearly still going up, to our skeptical delectation.

It was inevitable in this world of stacking your playthings that playing with angles—skewed stacking—would come next. The

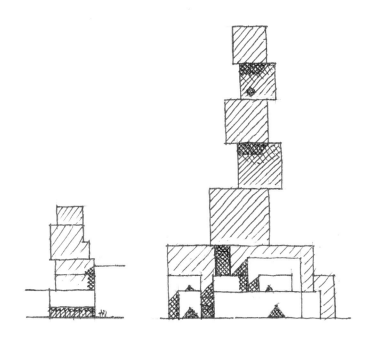

2.10 The New Museum, NYC; Foshan Opera Tower, Foshan, China

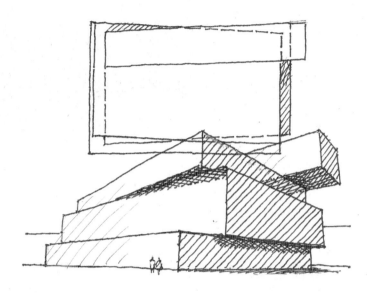

2.11 Halifax Central Library, Nova Scotia, Canada

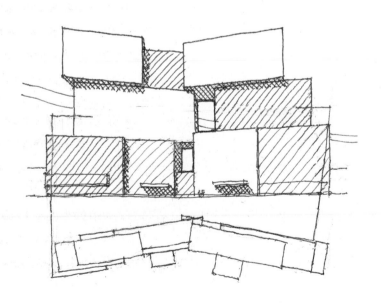

2.12 MGM Cotai Resort, Macau, China

Halifax, Nova Scotia Central Library, by Schmidt Hammer Lassen, stacks its glassy, colorful rectangular volumes at slight angles (Fig. 2.11). Do they bother us? Slight angles in elevation can be wince inducing, with the sharp pinch of converging lines and the ambiguity of what is horizontal, but in plan, one must admit they can have a sort of insouciant elegance. Shifting locales and scales drastically, KPF's massive MGM Cotai casino hotel in Macau deals with a stack of many boxes but just one angle, a shallow bend in its footprint beyond which the composition employs slight shifts to achieve an almost dignified composition (if it is even permitted to describe anything in Macau as remotely dignified) (Fig. 2.12).

One thing leading, as it often does, to another, we also find such stacks sporting more substantial angles, as at a boldly conceived public school in Virginia by BIG. Calling to mind the swing-out drawers of Joe Columbo's taboret, five levels dramatically fan out from a common "pivot point," as opposed to the subtly randomized skewing of the Halifax project (Fig. 2.13). The conceit results in some measure of structural complexity as the price for being eye-catching without notable functional advantage. A ways down the road one can see superficial similarities in Steven Holl's Institute for Contemporary Art at Virginia Commonwealth University. But with only two layers in the configuration, it doesn't become a compellingly iterative motif, and the bar-shaped wings, being subsidiary appendages to the taller frontal elements, are an aspect of the composition rather than *the* composition. The project as a whole is both more artful and less predictable as a result.

. . .

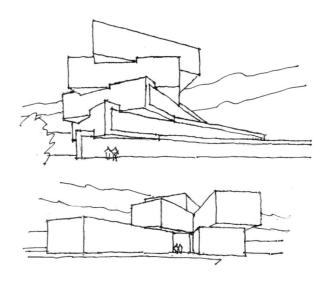

2.13 Wilson Secondary School, Arlington, VA;
Institute for Contemporary Art, VCU, Richmond, VA

If there are issues with stacking such similar elements, what of a jenga pile on steroids where, in contrast, every piece is a different shape, and at a different angle to every adjacent element, and all clad differently? MVRDV has designed such a project—the "Peruri 88" mixed use development—for Jakarta (Fig. 2.14). It actually seems almost all right (I think that was a Robert Venturi catch phrase), because its rather cheerful effect doesn't depend on seeming about to tip over, or at least not too much, and the variegated and exhilarating gaps and junctions seem worth the effort. Here the previous "disjunction of similar elements" via stacking them has come full circle to one of a "confluence of disparate elements" by truly bringing things together in three-dimensional space.

Rather surprisingly, the various approaches to treating a building as a stack of smaller buildings come off pretty well in this tiny sample. The exception of the Opera Cube Tower simply tells us that pushing the conceit to a scary extent seems a bit irresponsible.

True, there are all sorts of deliberately scary structures—cantilevered over cliff edges, hanging to the side of more conventional high-rises—but when the whole deal is about one unnerving hat trick, we are firmly on unfirm grounds of peculiarity.

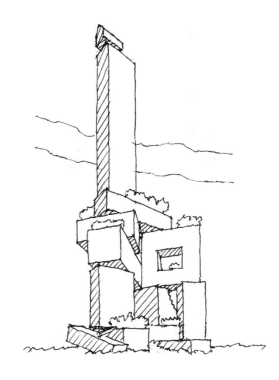

2.14 Peruri 88, Jakarta, Indonesia (Basic Massing)

2c. Exfoliating: Façade Disassembled

Perhaps this title seems a bit too closely related to skin care products, but it turns out to be uniquely descriptive of a particular set of architectural oddities, pretty much all having cropped up in our troubling century. Looking for precedents, the best examples would seem to be a plethora of ruins: Tintern Abbey, the Parthenon, the Hiroshima Atomic Bomb Dome: exfoliated all by the depredations of time, vandalism, or major explosives. In our current findings though, by and large the pieces are still here, just rearranged somewhat from their visualized "originating reality."

Planar Bits Fallout

The approach of "exfoliation" shows up in a variety of ways, in a sequence represented here as greater and greater degrees of effect. At the modest level of a grid of façade cladding panels, we find schemes base on designing them as if weakly attached, or as if not attached at all. Applications of some proprietary wall panels respond to an apparent concern that a blank wall is in need of visual incident (we recall the questionable resorts to variegated metal panel colorings), here featuring a square grid of flat panels flapping out in various directions: not too much, just enough to give the impression they may be flying away in the next breeze (Fig. 2.15). This also implies, unintentionally, a product that comes with an attachment detail more than willing to fail.

A different manifestation shows up in such distantly removed locales as Melbourne's Federation Square, by Bates Smart and others, and Calgary's Central Library by Snøhetta and DIALOG, wherein the grid is now a good deal more complex. In both cases, an artfully varied selection of panels, in several of the

2.15 Metal Panel Variant: "Flapping Out"

grid's irregular polygonal shapes, comes up missing (Fig. 2.16). An impression can be readily summoned up that the complicated grid has made the job of properly attaching all those differently shaped panels a bit too arduous and that they've blown away in the wind. Vivid imagery aside, the reality is that these represent another shot at the quintessential dilemma of the window, to wit, the way they're always cropping up and becoming either a dull repetitive pattern or an obtrusively irregular one. The conceit in these cases may be that if the entire façade is an irregular grid, the fact that some panels are transparent will end up seeming more artful than more random.

Incremental Uncoupling

The above are "paper-thin" approaches to the brave new theme of a façade that appears to be coming apart, in that the façade remains and it's the relatively small and conceptually two-dimensional elements that are peeling away or vanishing. Amping up to a more robust coming-apart level, a significant trend seems to have arisen involving the vertical segments that a building façade is bound to consist of—whether revealed or concealed—and imposing some alternating "flip-flopping." The main motive, presumably, is an activated and dimensionally expressive surface, but a seemingly unavoidable consequence is the impression that fairly large elements are detaching themselves from the building face. The outward bends imply an effect of axial compression, as if the assembly had been overheated or overstressed by said compression and had to give, popping these joints outward in a semi-random way. Sacramento's Golden 1 Center by AECOM, an

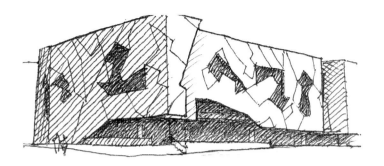

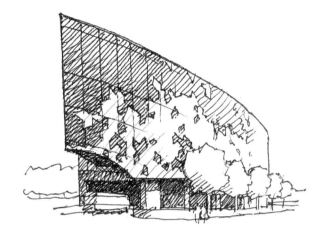

2.16 Federation Square, Melbourne, Victoria, Australia; Calgary Central Library, Alberta, Canada

arena, applies the motif at a large scale with alternating segments advancing and receding, as well as featuring an awkward corner cutout for the entrance (Fig. 2.17.1). Why awkward? An exterior treatment such as this which just keeps going, as opposed to being somehow articulated in subsections, will look like someone took a bread knife to it and carved out a piece when interrupted in this way. A similar morphology appears in Dominique Perrault's façade rework at New Mechanics Hall, Ecole Polytechnique Fédérale de Lausanne, but in the form of flip-flopping panels of metal mesh, and an elaborate contraption incorporating canopies at the entrance furthers the sense that a collapse is not only imminent but underway (Fig. 2.17.2). A metaphor of a woven fabric may

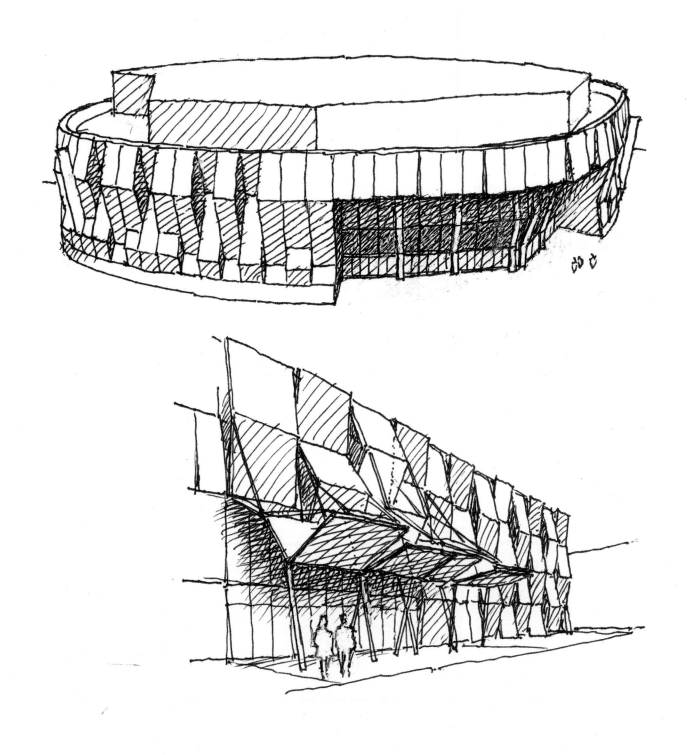

2.17.1 Golden 1 Center, Sacramento, CA
2.17.2 New Mechanics Hall, École Polytechnique Fédérale de Lausanne, Switzerland

have a conscious part in these sorts of efforts, but weaving involves both weft and warp: since only warp is present, one could visualize that the above are uncoupling due to not being fully "woven."

Who knows, maybe basket weaving is a better metaphor, the stiffness and thickness of reeds resulting in a more dimensional surface that is also fully woven. Rather unfortunately, facades based on this this look have become a bit of a thing, an online search for "building facades that appear woven" revealing any number of generally bumpy finds, some of which truly adopt the appearance if not the reality of both weft and warp. In such cases, this chapter's theme—a sense that things are uncoupling—is defused, sort of, by a façade having taken up the general look of a wicker basket, should that be deemed a desirable result for some reason. A project in Turkey demonstrates one intrinsic potential problem with such a consistently repeating pattern, recalling the above bread knife reference at awkward truncations where wider openings are called for (Fig. 2.18).

Facade Uncoupling

Facades that are detached from their buildings have been a modernist commonplace, appearing as everything from Le Corbusier's brise soleils to ubiquitous screens and scrims of perforated metal standing free of an actual wall. And in truth these elements are often eminently defensible, both as formative expression and in serving the useful purpose of controlling solar insolation. This "category" is not meant to include the sort of thing that Rietveld did in his Schröder house or Mies in his unbuilt country houses or Barcelona Pavilion (sort of), namely to develop a building as something of a house of cards. Such projects aren't expressive of coming apart; they are in pieces already, sui generis. A related and enduring design trope mixes in "blade walls," either as stand-alone insertions or boundary wall extensions, to articulate architectural compositions. This is not façade uncoupling but dimensional salad, a spicing up of the three- dimensional elements we have come to find boring with such quasi two-dimensional accents.

Instead, our interest here is piqued by whole facades that appear to have once been securely part of the building wrapper, but which have pulled away or slipping sideways or both. The approach has ample precedents in the preceding century, as at Stanley Tigerman's Regional Library for Chicago or the Pei firm's addition to the Portland Museum of Art (Fig. 2.19). But while these are essentially expressive of solid walls that have disconnected, recent cases exploit the surreal effect of a big wall of glass that's come loose, as at Krueck and Sexton's FBI South Florida Headquarters (Fig. 2.20). It features glass curtainwalls extending well beyond the sides and top, plus an articulation so as to appear spaced outboard of the building face. Thus these outboard facades are singled out for exfoliation, paying homage to a persistent urge to express architectural form as simultaneously volumetric and planar. And it bears noting in this case that the building ensemble is made to appear lifted above the ground plane, further emphasizing a theme of uncoupling. (The equally notable "pleated" treatment of this project's end facades will get some attention later.)

2.18 Argül Weave, Bursa, Turkey

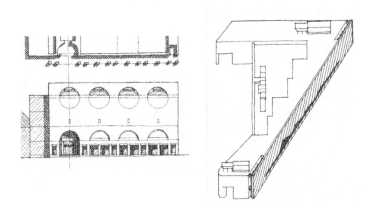

2.19 Portland Museum of Art, ME;
Former Illinois Regional Library for the Blind and
Physically Handicapped, Chicago

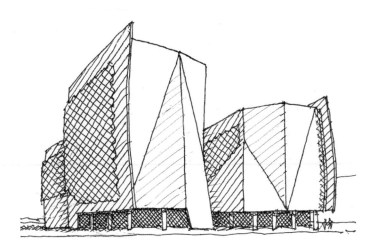

2.20 FBI South Florida Headquarters, Miramar, FL

Whole Shooting Match Uncoupling Via Simulated Effect of Major Explosives

A final step would be for all facades to uncouple, all at once. Gehry Partners is the chief in this department. LA's Disney Hall, Bilbao's Guggenheim, Paris's Fondation Louis Vuitton—all exhibit, to varying degrees, a sense that the pieces have all disconnected and are flying apart in all directions (Fig. 2.21). In some cases, the pieces are convex, evoking spinnakers, while others are concave, as if blown out from the side rather than the center. While the Fondation visibly comprises outer sails and inner building volumes—that mix of two-and three-dimensional elements again, now on steroids—Disney Hall is all flying potato chips hiding any sense of the inner building. And the Guggenheim is a mix: flying flaps and petals in the front, mingled with solid boxes in the back.

It's a big step from the gimmick of a single uncoupled façade, generally remaining parallel to its originating volume, to this one, of curved planes flying apart in all directions. What of an intermediate step in the progression- a family of detached facades that hasn't been blown into spinnakers? Such things don't seem to be showing up much as a thing in this century, excepting some expensive and possibly unlivable residential projects. And indeed those "house of cards" exemplars— the Barcelona Pavilion, the Schröder House, distinctly impractical constructs ahead of their time—were themselves residential in scale. To emulate the image of an "explosion in a shingle factory" (a disparaging description once made of a painting by Duchamp)—is apparently hard to do—crazy, really—at a large building scale. But I'll bet they're out there, somewhere.

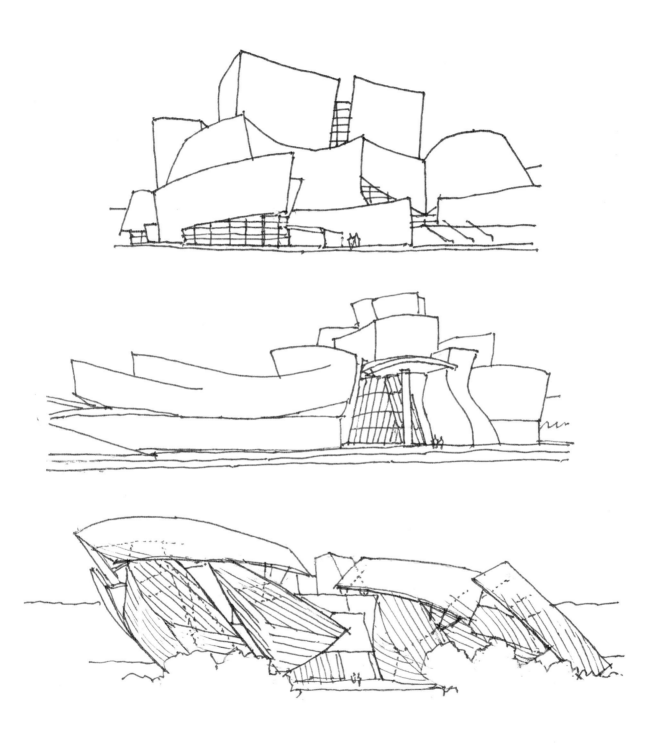

2.21 Walt Disney Concert Hall, Los Angeles; Guggenheim Museum Bilbao, Spain;
Fondation Louis Vuitton, Paris

"Fragmentation": A Summary

These three tales have dealt with some of the more conventional 21st century means to increase the complexity of a basic design, being different approaches to "breakage." **Stratifying** takes the intrinsic resource of multistory buildings as a stack of platforms and develops it via the conceptual application of axial forces. **Complicating** employs the imagined dis- and re-assembly of a basic design, to result in a confluence of elements, either similar or dissimilar. And **exfoliating** takes an initiating shape and conceptually applies *outward* forces, causing its boundaries to disassemble. Disassembly is the watchword of these approaches, resulting in an increase in the number of architectonic pieces and parts by their various means. Such breakage is not necessarily a bad thing, but as we have found, it may often be easier to get it wrong than to get it better.

It can appear at this juncture as if brave new designers out there got that message and set out to do it differently: to fool with the thing without doing those types of obvious damage. But ironically, the results ended up often doing damage of even more obvious and peculiar varieties.

DEFORMATION: SHAPE CHANGED BY DISTORTION

The preceding approaches of breaking up a basic shape to increase its morphological interest actually have some substantial precedents. In light of this, it does seem likely that designers aspiring to avant-garde status would want to try something a little more new and nifty, without the risks of familiarity that come with those precedents. So what to do? A popular answer seems to be to take the basic form that the project wants to be and mess with it: stretch it, twist it, shove it, push it over. Not wholly without precedents either, to be sure, but more boldly focused on one hard-to-miss "move:" a little formative ultraviolence.

3a. Stretching: Skyscrapers, Groundscrapers

The presence of "stretching" in architecture's past is there if you look for it. Gothic church towers featuring spires can seem attenuated by having been stretched upward. Some Norwegian stave churches consist of a recursive stack of elements that become taller and thinner. In modern times we note the attenuative qualities of stepped back art deco towers, and, a bit more recently, the rather too obvious effects of a few tall facades that feature sweeping upward concavities (Fig. 3.1).

While less obvious, precedents evoking "lateral" stretching are also out there. Some probably unintentional examples could include the bell tower of Hawksmoor's Christ Church Spitalfields, stretched to fully enfront the nave beyond, or the longitudinal profile of Aalto's Finlandia Hall, thinning out toward the middle as if stretched like taffy. Or dare one question an aspect of Kahn's canonized Kimbell Art Museum, its pair of porches so very elongated—stretched, almost—between the comparatively skinny columns at the ends (Fig. 3.2).

As a more general thing, lateral stretching has appeared as sweeping transverse concavities that can evoke a project stretched to serve the limits of its site and program. But none of this was likely to have been conscious precedent for the following:

Stretching Up

The phenomenon of very tall buildings is well enough known, although I guess that depends on the background of the reader. Architects and urbanists are covered up with publications and websites that keep them abreast, at least superficially, of the steady onset of architectural tallness. Supertall buildings—defined as those between 300 and 600 meters in height—are planned, underway or in existence all over the world, perhaps most notably in China, the Arabian Peninsula, and Southeast Asia. Although the Empire State Building was the world's tallest building until 1970 at 380 m, by far the largest number of these supertalls are being planned or built in the 21st century, including upwards of 30 in Manhattan alone.

Once those became sort of commonplace, "megatall" buildings, up to a kilometer in height, became the next pointless goal. Among those currently planned, that goal will be reached by one, the Kingdom Tower in Jeddah, once completed (Fig. 3.3). The Burj Khalifa in Dubai (a mere 828 m tall) and others are built or under construction in Shanghai, Mecca, Kuala Lumpur, Bangkok, and elsewhere. They are uniformly variations on attempted sleek modernism, and indeed a good many are expressive of "stretching," their profiles thinning out as they rise. (Exceptions bear noting, including the bunch-o-sharp-points treatment atop Jakarta's planned Signature Tower, and a massive traditional design of surpassing clumsiness in Mecca.)

Did I say pointless? Well, they are, really. To be sure, there is some theorizing around and about that tall and very tall buildings are good in basic ways: they take the place of a sprawl of lower buildings, they're profitable for developers if you

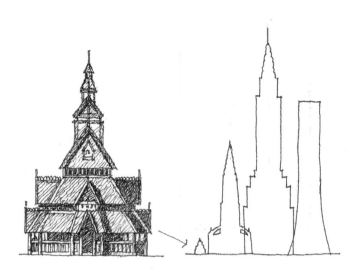

3.1 Borgund Stave Church, Norway, and Profiles of Borgund Stave Church; Ulm Minster, Germany; Chrysler Building, NYC; Solow Building, NYC

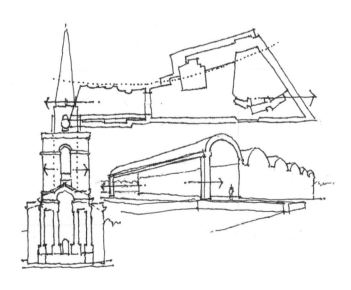

3.2 Christ Church Spitalfields, London; Finlandia Hall, Helsinki; Kimbell Art Museum, Fort Worth, TX

call that an advantage, they afford some mighty nice views, and, well, I'm sure there are other advantages. But there are a few corresponding disadvantages, among them low floor efficiencies due to all the elevators, difficult issues of seismic forces and wind turbulence, access and public safety concerns, cost premiums, extra demands on civic infrastructure, sustainability issues—you get the idea.

On the face of it there would appear to be three overarching forces leading to the proliferation of tall and very tall buildings. One might logically wonder whether urban development pressures due to overpopulation are a factor in urban densification generally, helping to push up the supertalls. The world has a good many more people than it ought to, surely a passable assertion with 7.5 billion and barreling headlong toward a "physical maximum" of 10 billion. (The world's population in 1960 was 3 billion.) But this matter is somewhat off topic, and anyway, all things considered, maybe the planet has begun to take matters a bit more into its own hands as far as dealing with this increasingly itchy fungus on its epidermis is concerned.

In reality two other issues are more likely to be at fault. A combo of ready capital and technological advances is one, and surely the other is simply ego: it feels cool to have built something so absurdly tall, and it evidently feels cool to live there. Or not: one thinks in particular of the "splinter" buildings that have ruined Manhattan's midtown skyline, which are all about oligarchs and other hyper-rich who need a place to launder some money, or to simply have on hand to flip later, or to move into if things go south in the homeland, leaving their many-million-dollar condos vacant much or all of the time. Or maybe a lot of them are just empty,

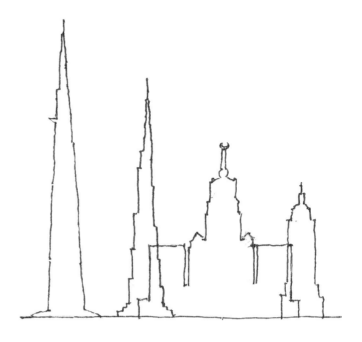

3.3 Kingdom Tower, Jeddah, Saudi Arabia; Burj Khalifa, Dubai, UAE; Abraj Al Bait, Mecca, Saudi Arabia; Empire State Building, NYC

period, as economies and politics continue to mess things up by changing all the time. These places are super skinny as well as super tall, for engineering can and does achieve wonders nowadays, but the results are disproportionate and unnerving. Awe is not the emotion they evoke: it's more something like repellence, as with a grotesque invasive plant sprouting up on your property.

In *A Pattern Language*, Christopher Alexander opined that four stories really ought to be as tall as buildings get, with a few exceptions: you know, something the reasonably fit could climb with no difficulty, and from which you are able to see activities outside, and to be seen. A silly idea, some may say, but it has a lot going for it. Too bad it's too late.

Stretching Out

The cutesy term "groundscraper" has been coined for the phenomenon of something along the lines of a skyscraper in size that lies down on the ground instead. Of course, such great big long buildings have long existed—factories, for a prime example—so they aren't quite as odd as something a kilometer tall. There's a particular subtype, though, that's of interest, wherein a relatively low-rise building stretches out in *all* directions to sometimes questionable degrees. "Pancake" would be a more apt moniker. These can be criticized, as can anything, but by and large their great big carpets of roof seem almost defensible, the more so to the degree that roof openings and skylights mitigate a sense of entering a labyrinth of dim caverns beneath. Best to leave the subject as a lightly annotated list (Fig. 3.4):

- National Kaohsiung Center for the Arts: Taiwan: Mecanoo: 740' long and almost as wide. Dim, monochrome, cavernous interstitial caveways amongst the venues seem a harsh price to pay for the gimmick of the great big square wavy roof.

- Rolex Learning Center: École Polytechnique Fédérale de Lausanne: SANAA: Another big square single undulating space, but well equipped with roundish lightwells and courtyards. Both of these seem a bit expressive of having been laid down and stretched over some bumpy pre-existing elements, resulting in the wavy profiles. Monochrome. Ok, so what's the rule against color in these flatbreads? Perhaps their architects happened to be among that large majority who are simply afraid of it?

- National Library: Qatar: OMA: Grinning, squashed lozenges comprise three of the four very long elevations, seemingly teetering on their bottom points. Partially redeemed by the interesting but inefficient-looking great big single public space. The presence of books (of all things) helps ameliorate the all-white interior.

- McCormick Tribune Campus Center: IIT: OMA: While not remotely in the league of the above in scale terms, the building is still pretty big, managing to become a largish labyrinth with its angled passages and angular light courts. At last, substantial colorfulness does appear. The project manages to also embody another and rather unique morphological type, that of the lightly crushed flattish building, being deliberately bent at the middle in order to pass under the bypassing L train. This seems pretty unconscionable, being both silly looking and a taunting affront to the surrounding Miesian campus. Yes, the place did need some variety, but really-

- Apple Park: Cupertino: Foster: Not along the lines of the above at all, but notable as a (curvi) linear groundscraper: the enormous doughnut will present a morphological problem should it come time to make additions. Its diameter is over twice the length of the Taiwan Arts Center.

One aspect of this approach to architecture that is just a little bit unsettling is that it faintly reminds one of the genre of "encapsulated civilizations" in novels, movies, etc.: "Dark City," "THX 1138," *Caves of Steel, The Dark Forest,* and much else: in short, a retreat from the harsh real world into an extensive manmade one, often grim and, yes, monochrome.

44

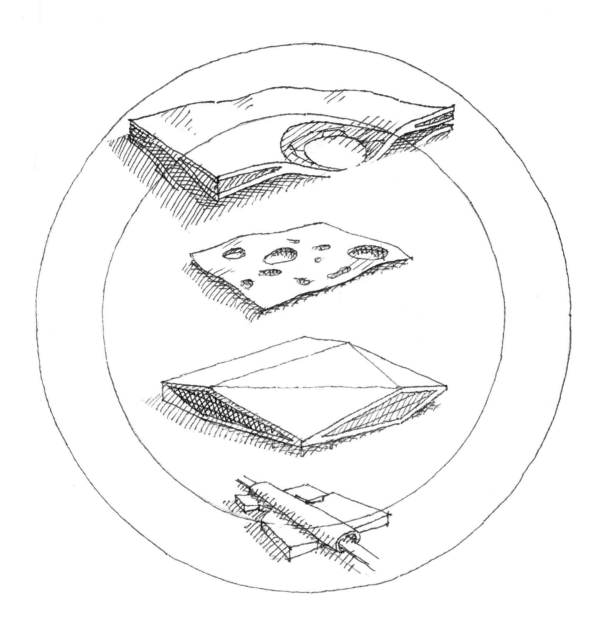

3.4 Sandwich Fixin's: National Kaohsiung Center for the Arts, Taiwan; Rolex Learning Center, Lausanne; Qatar National Library, Doha; McCormick Tribune Campus Center, Chicago; Apple Park, Cupertino, CA (Footprint)

3b. Tilting:
Variations on a Theme of Out of Plumb

That catch-all title refers to building designs with significant aspects that are neither vertical nor horizontal. Sloping roofs, long a commonplace, need not detain us too much; less common and often less defensible applications of the slanting surface are the matters of interest. As with "stretching," a taking apart in pieces doesn't occur, but distortions of a variety of angled natures do. Hopefully this examination of "tilting" will not be too much in the way of tilting at windmills—

Precedents

Looking back, Pisa's leaning tower is certainly tilting, but no one expected it to tilt nor has it inspired future tilted cylinders, though ironically Pisan tourism has surely exceeded what it would have been otherwise. Further back, the world's various pyramids are nothing *but* tilts, making them something of a special case. Battered and buttressed walls recur throughout history as direct expressions of the need to keep from tipping over, including the ultimate case of high dams for hydroelectric power and flood control (Fig. 3.5). (Many of these dams are admirable works of architectonic form as well as engineering: some of the TVA dams were designed, to be sure with a lot of engineering support, by an architect.)

Moving up to the late decades of the past century, the pyramid is back, for some reason, in Memphis, Las Vegas, Paris, and elsewhere. In Dallas, the Pei firm's Allied Bank Tower (now Fountain Place) features a semi-pyramidal top—a gable, really, a startlingly scaleless skyline—which might be said to have opened up the subject of "tilts with issues" (Fig. 3.6). The main body of the building is actually a

3.5 Norris Dam, Tennessee

parallelogram, hardly perceivable as such and with no particular urban rationale, as opposed to the possibly defensible similar footprint of the same firm's John Hancock tower, now 200 Clarendon Street, in Boston. (One may decry the latter's enormously outsize scale, but the skewed footprint at least presented its narrower face toward Copley Square and opened up a plaza across from Trinity Church.) The Dallas case's issues of arbitrarily tilting geometry and arbitrary urban form provide a prescient foretaste of tilting applications to come in the current century.

Tilted Soffits or the Illusion Thereof

As we have found, a notable aspect of modernism nowadays is the ceaseless search for a new angle (literally, in the case of the present discussion). Roofs have been tilted all sorts of ways for ages, of course, and walls, well, their notable departures from the vertical will be addressed soon enough. Building undersides, though, all else being fiddled with, soon came to be mined for tilting opportunities as well, whether as "honest expressionism" or just something new. The LA museum "The Broad," by DS+R, tilts up the corners of its elaborate concrete scrim, but actually there is no soffit and this is more of a pulling up of the skirts: a completely different let's-explore-the-mysterious-caves condition is revealed once ducking under the corners, so the underside tilt is just a nominally a two-dimensional one in this case. For an actual realization, way back near the exhilarating start of his career James Stirling brought forth the Engineering Building at Leicester, and its forthrightly modeled lecture

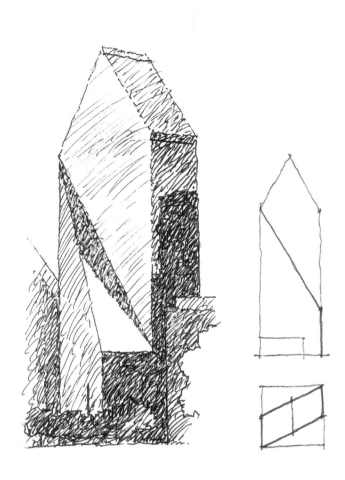

3.6 Fountain Place, Dallas

hall elements featured the real thing in terms of sloped soffits. (Figs. 3.7, 3.8).

Since programmatic elements that are likely to show up in buildings simply don't include very much in the way of tilting floors, such steeply raked auditoriums or lecture halls are pretty much the main grist for this mill. It is also now de rigueur in academic buildings of this century to have "bleacher steps" or something of the sort, in order to sit while killing time with one's device and having the opportunity to observe nothing in particular (No field games inside yet, just ping-pong, sometimes): raked lecture halls without the hall or the lecture. One of each of

47

3.7 The Broad, Los Angeles

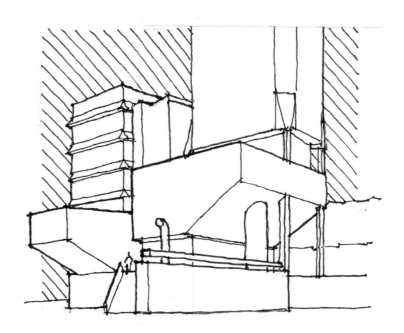

3.8 Engineering Faculty Building, Leicester, UK

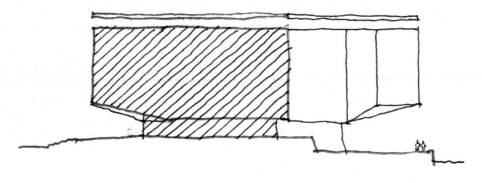

3.9 Tata Center, Cornell Tech, NYC: Diagrammatic Section/Elevation

these types is to be found in the Tata Center for Technology and Design at Cornell Tech, Weiss Manfredi's strange bedfellow neighbor of the previously observed Bloomberg Center, permitting somewhat chunky sloping soffit realizations in a somewhat chunky project, earnestly developed but seemingly too big for its britches (or site) (Fig. 3.9). More later on the Cornell Tech master plan. And when you go, expecting to also trek down to Lou Kahn's FDR memorial, remember it's closed on Tuesdays—

Another NYC sloped soffit, but one called for by no particular programmatic function, appears in DS+R's newish front end of the Juilliard School at Lincoln Center (Fig. 3.10). Now there's nothing wrong in principle with an expressive gesture such as this: the uplifting of space below can be exhilarating, the hope perhaps being to evoke a generous, expansive sensibility. But its appearance in this case also seems almost a gesture of contempt for Catalano and Belluschi's rather classy building, not flaw-free but surely the best of the otherwise pretty bad lot making up Lincoln Center (ok, Saarinen/

Hardy's fine work also excepted). The Juilliard addition, though, does everything it can to thumb its nose at the husky aesthetic of the original, breaking its horizontals, making fun of its windows, and dragging its dignified sense of solidity forward to some pasted-together frontal corners possessing no sense of dimensional depth whatsoever. So here's a tilted soffit that does make for a nice space below it, but which turns around and does damage to the building it enfronts.

Partially Tilting

The feeling that something may be tipping over is a fundamental issue to ponder when dealing in "tilting" as an architectural bright idea. So many buildings are so tall and skinny nowadays that we've become accustomed to what should be an unnerving impression that they can't possibly continue staying straight up that way. To add some visual stability—once a reasonable enough goal—one logical gesture would be to slope one building face to serve architectonically as a "buttress" for the straight

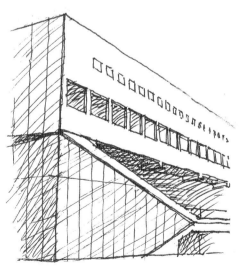

3.10 Juilliard School, NYC: Renovation/Addition

49

up remainder. Say what you will about the Empire State Plaza at Albany, NY, and many bad things have been and should be said, its row of four office towers does achieve this effect, the buttress-like element engaging the wider main body plus extending above it to enhance the effect (though one wishes for something—anything at all—to make the end product the least bit interesting) (Fig. 3.11).

More recently, in the nightmare architectonic playground of downtown London, we see that Rogers Stirk Harbour's 122 Leadenhall Street, forever to be known as the Cheesegrater, detaches its slope-sided buttress and turns it into the whole building, the connected vertical element being simply the elevator and restroom core (and pretty snazzy elevators and restrooms they are) (Fig. 3.12). The latter being both shorter and narrower than the bigger wedge, the former appears to be forever tipping over backwards from some angles, ironically *reversing* the image of a buttress strengthening against failure.

A pertinent comparison can be made with a particular aspect of Manhattan's Hudson Yards, the massive development called a "supersized suburban-style office park" by the New York Times, namely of the prominent pair of glassy towers by KPF. Boiled down to essentials, their predominant vertical faces are outboard, while sloping faces look at each other across the intervening one-percenter shopping mall, getting farther away from each other on the way up (Fig. 3.13). The effect is particularly pronounced seen from the southwest, being an illusion of tipping over, and, diabolically, the chamfered-off tops add to the impression. So yet again the image (intentional or not) of a sloping face having a visually strengthening

3.11 Empire State Plaza, Albany, NY: Office Buildings

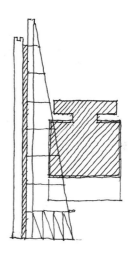
3.12 122 Leadenhall Street, London

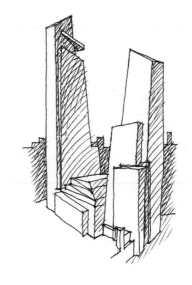
3.13 Hudson Yards, NYC

effect on the overall massing, seems to have achieved the very opposite.

. . .

In this matter of "partial tilting" it would be negligent to fail to address the opposite and far more logic-defying case wherein a face of a tall building slopes *out* on the way up. Counterintuitive, yes, but certain to be eye-catching, which has become a primary requirement in this morphologically lawless age. BIG's Vancouver House apartments had a difficult triangular site, so to maximize leasable area the building perimeter transitions upward incrementally from a triangle at the base to a rectangle at the top (Fig.3.14). The impact from some vantage points is startling, with precious little building seeming available to support the top-heavy and overhanging upper levels: in other words, it does indeed look ready to tip over at any moment. (And strictly speaking this sloping façade is actually a doubly curved one, thus a foretaste of the section to follow on "warping.")

Less unbelievable outward slopes have been essayed over the years: Pei's Dallas City Hall looms out ominously on one long face, as does M. Jeanneret-Gris's Youth and Cultural Center at Firminy (Fig. 3.15). And having mentioned modern-day pyramids earlier, one recalls there are a number of upside-down pyramids out there, findable via Google by the morbidly curious. These are oddities both intrinsically and in that they are few: the outward tilt idea just doesn't lend itself to either structural logic (though that seems to matter little nowadays) or to visual comfort.

Tilted Tops

As noted, roofs have been tilting throughout history: originally to shed the rain, and more

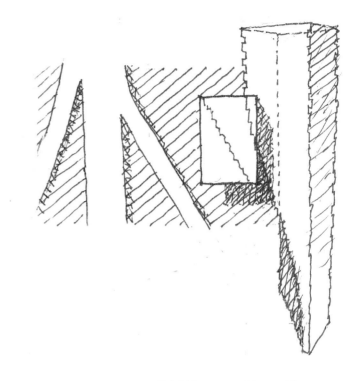

3.14 Vancouver House, Vancouver

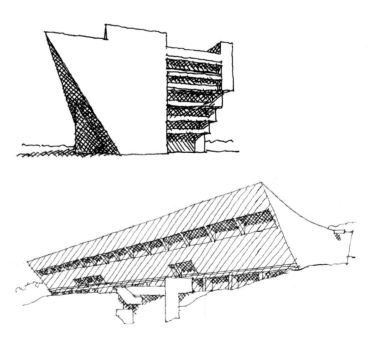

3.15 City Hall, Dallas; Youth and Cultural Center, Firminy, France

51

frequently, well, it's still the preferred way to keep the rain out, but also as one more way to try to be new and different. And it's a lot more readily achieved than tilting the walls or the floors. Expressively, tilted tops make intuitive sense to us: a combination of an expression of the erosive forces of nature with a sense that the heavens have been stormed a bit. (Though one must admit such an image is arguably best expressed by an incremental diminution of the top, as on what remains to this day the best-looking tall building, the Empire State.) All that said, customary gables, hips, sheds, butterflies, etc. need not detain us; we seek tilted rooftops that aid or abet the notably peculiar. It's true that tall buildings do get slanted tops occasionally, as at Chicago's Crain Communications, Dallas' Fountain Place, or Manhattan's Citicorp Center, but these earnest precedents don't quite qualify (Fig. 3.16).

We've seen them appear at Hudson Yards, so how about a look at the other preeminently enormous Manhattan project of this century so far, the Ground Zero development. Not that you will find them there as built (excepting Foster's reinstated Two WTC design with its aggressive bundle-o-chisels profile or whatever is eventually built). That aside, only on Daniel Libeskind's competition-winning master plan for Ground Zero does one see deferentially and raffishly tilted tops, angling down to corners rather than eaves, the entire ensemble spiraling around to the apotheosis of the tallest tower paired with its gardens-in-the-sky steeple-spear (said to be an abstract redux of the Statue of Liberty's raised arm and torch) (Fig. 3.17.1). This ensemble of tilts, along with the eye-catching and clearly never-to-be-really tilted mullion grids, plus that spear, may have been among the winning attributes of the scheme (along with the fact that the other schemes,

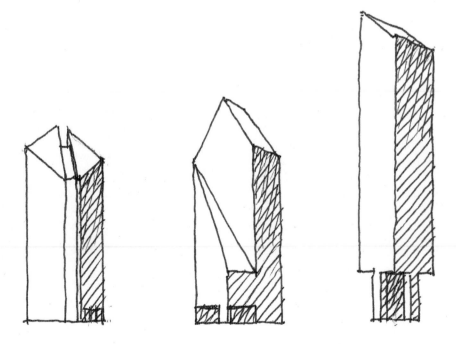

3.16 Crain Communications Building, Chicago; Fountain Place, Dallas; Citicorp Center, NYC

52

with the possible exception of those by Foster and Peterson Littenberg, were, not to put too fine a point on it, laughably inept, especially given that a presumably blue ribbon panel of starchitects had been tapped to take their best shot).

A torturous history of incremental whittling away at the winning master plan resulted, such that one can only feel a bit sorry for Libeskind, bless his heart, despite his scheme's shortcomings. Leaving aside the politics of the matter, the big shots moved in and flattened the tops, straightened out the sites, and turned the super-duper spear thing into the sort of glass obelisk often found on coffee tables of the nouveau riche (Fig.3.17.2). So in this case the peculiarly tilting top served as a straw dog, questionable to begin with but rather sadly missed in comparison to what we got instead.

Leaning

There is a sequence of sorts to this subject of tilting. We've seen cases of soffits angling up, sidewalls angling over (this way or that way), and roofs tilting down in unexpected ways; the next step may be to throw caution to the winds and simply lean the whole thing sideways. This runs the risk of being a sort of cheap trick (though not cheap in terms of the structural framing required), but undoubtedly an attention-grabber. A leaning building again recalls Pisa's Tower, way out of plumb and (repeating ourselves) looking as if it might tip over at any moment, but since it doesn't, it's a deliberate look-at-me gesture. Madrid's "Gate of Europe," dating from the '90's and from Philip Johnson's "let's take a shot at cool modernism next" phase, was an early harbinger of this sort of thing, the paired office towers

3.17.1 Ground Zero Master Plan, Early Concept

3.17.2 WTC As Being Built

53

leaning toward each other in a sort of implied mutual support (Fig. 3.18.1).

A next step in a sequence, one of bringing the two leaners out of alignment, will remove that sense of support, and this is seemingly the case of the aptly named Veer Towers by Murphy/ Jahn at Las Vegas' "City Center" (Fig. 3.18.2). These condo buildings with their parallelogram footprints are side by side and "veer" in opposite directions. As a result there is no mutual leaning toward; if anything they lean away, in a sliding sideways sort of way, that seems specifically designed to bewilder. But that said, their close proximity almost results in the impression of a single building as seen from the boulevard, the opposed leanings resulting in a different sort of "holding each other up" via the implication of a shared stable foundation. This, as well as their proximity to Libeskind's "Shops at Crystals" (said crystals evidently having fallen from a very high place) and backgrounded by variously sweeping and swooping high-rises, renders them almost an anchor of stability after all.

If we go to the next, next step—a building that leans all by itself with no buddy to figuratively share the painful shear and moment forces— there aren't that many to be found, which is perhaps understandable. But if we back down from this ode to leaning high-rises, another look at Hadid's Broad Art Museum in the wilds of Michigan (not to be confused with the art museum named The Broad in LA) is called for (Fig. 3.19). It's being pushed, pulled, or both, blown over as if a great plains wind had found its way a little farther north than usual. But compared to the amorphous context of the above leaners, the Broad directly adjoins some strait-laced Collegiate Gothic which it clearly doesn't much like, its sharp edges thrusting in

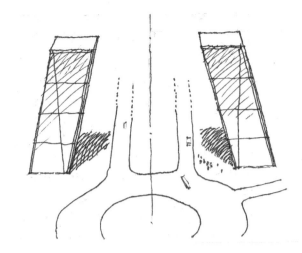

3.18.1 Gate of Europe, Madrid

3.18.2 Veer Towers, Las Vegas

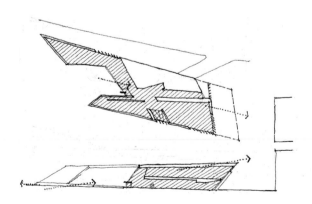

3.19 Eli and Edythe Broad Art Museum, Michigan State University

that direction, a portion of its baffling montage of pleated paneling resembling a wide-open maw, complete with sharp teeth (Fig. 1.9). Not only do the building's opposite shorter faces lean in parallel, a tilted top is prominently in evidence as well, further emphasizing the sense of directional thrust, for the project exemplifies stretching as well as tilting. The Broad simply seems to have landed in the wrong place: it looks like an embedded shard of something about to come loose that belongs on a vast prairie somewhere instead of a handy vacant lot.

Bent

Toronto's less aggressively formed low-rise Albion Library by Perkins & Will recalls the tilted soffit, with each corner of the roughly square building pulled up at an angle from a centerline fulcrum (Fig. 3.20). It's a pseudo-soffit case, though, as the walls and roof are doing the tipping, not the floor. Our purpose of harkening back to soffits is to bring to the fore the particular phenomenon of a building tilting in two directions at once, i.e., bent in the middle. A redux of the still reappearing mid-century butterfly roof comes to mind, but here we speak of the whole thing butterflied (albeit not really in this particular instance). The likelihood of such a shape seeming problematically teeter-tottery is mitigated in this case by the realities of columns and glasswalls extending to grade, and its very nature as a simulacrum speaks to the ultimate impracticality of a butterfly building with tilting floors as well as roofs, though I have no doubt they are out there.

Bent high-rise buildings are also a thing, as SHoP has done with Manhattan's American Copper condo buildings (Fig. 3.21). Vaguely

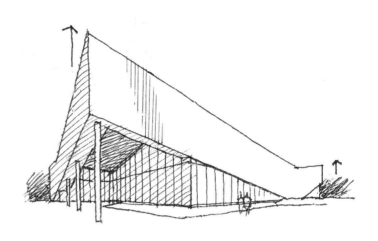

3.20 Albion District Library, Toronto

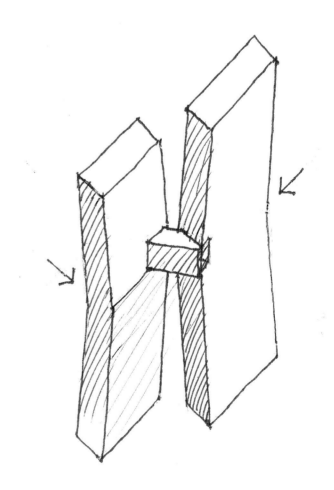

3.21 American Copper Building, NYC

55

recalling the veers, each of the two parallel and slipped-sideways towers bends outboard at the waist, one on the short side and the other on the long side. At that break point a skybridge linking the two diagonally manages to craft a roughly stabilized-looking ensemble, although some vantage points can't escape a bit of a stove-in quality. Is this a salutary innovation, or dare one ponder the alternative merits of straightening up the upper parts, thus "buttresses" below leading to orthogonal resolution above, as the better part of valor in the ongoing quest for the next new thing?

And one shouldn't leave the matter of bent buildings without harkening back to Gehry's Stata Center, with various of its tipsy village elements bent this way and that (Fig. 2.8). Our eye level view somewhat enhances the already over-enhanced impression of tipping over. Which leads us to the following:

Totally Tipping Over and Crashing About

Well, let's admit that what follows is the "centerpiece" of all this tilting business: as opposed to leaning, bending, etc., the full monty is to just go ahead and tip the whole thing over. And let's face it, Daniel Libeskind sort of owns this idea, for better or worse. Additions to three museums—San Francisco's Contemporary Jewish Museum, Toronto's Royal Ontario, and the Bundeswehr Military History Museum in Dresden—offer variations on one theme, being metallic prisms or collisions thereof, themselves colliding with the radically different historicist buildings that preceded them (Figs. 3.22). They also collide with the ground plane: sloped facets dive into it, there being no horizontal facets apparent on the exterior at all. Symbolism infusing the CJM addition is said to be hard to

discern, and its scattered little diamond windows look a bit like another case of "planar bits exfoliation." Both it and the Toronto project are, oddly enough, criticized by their curators for a notable lack of vertical walls on the interiors.

I had thought to compliment the Dresden project on the way that its single colliding arrowhead concisely distills war's horrors, but then I read that the intention was sort of the opposite: to contrast the arrowhead's transparency and openness with the old building's rigidity. To each his own, I suppose, in these deep and murky waters. Toronto's more complex collidive concatenation may do a better job of attracting and retaining one's interest, though if in a churlish mood some might say it's a bit like one's unwholesome interest in a bad wreck on the highway. While critics disagree on these projects' merits, there is general agreement that they are unnerving, harsh, and aggressive, and we are left with the hard-to-answer questions: did these communities and museums need such short, sharp shocks to awaken them and their visiting tourists (and bring income), and was it entirely fair for the existing museums to be put quite so violently into the background?

Ways That "Tilting" Has Sort of Worked

The thing about tilted architecture is that it can look like a bit of a joke, really: depending on the extremity of the expression, it leaves us with the question, was that really intentional? And since, well, there it is, so I guess it was, what was the purpose? One can go out on a rather short limb and generalize that the purpose was to gain attention, to be different, to exhibit some thinking outside the box, and, in the most extreme cases, to pretend to be an assertive art

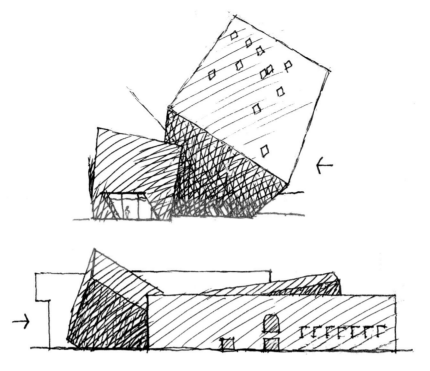

3.22.1 Contemporary Jewish Museum, San Francisco

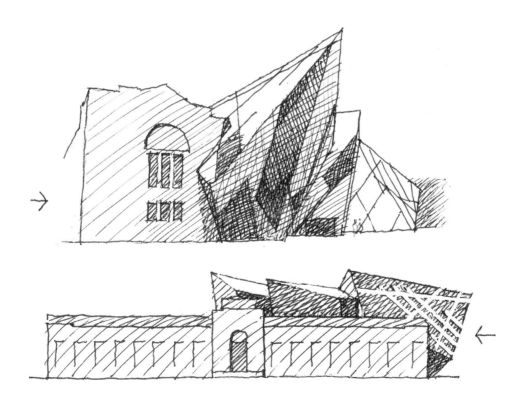

3.22.2 Royal Ontario Museum, Toronto

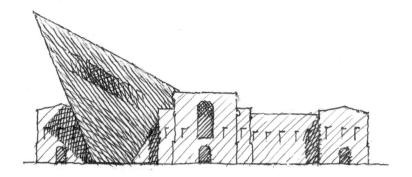

3.22.3 Bundeswehr Military History Museum, Dresden

object. Of course, being different is, in principle, often a good thing; if an extended ensemble of buildings (that would be, say, a city) were consistently tasteful and coordinated, that would be a mighty dull fate. And the converse— if everything was chaotically different from everything else—well, that would be really hard to do, but if achieved, would be a screaming dystopia, and there are several locales which have pretty much managed to do this that I have in mind and that you may as well.

Let's say we keep an eye out for applications of tilting that have merit beyond plain old shock value. What do we think, for example, about Piano's London "Shard" (Fig. 3.23.1)? Well, it's kind of conspicuously by itself with space all around it, seeming a bit out of place as it were, though the way London is going this may not be for long. As opposed to other projects with tilted walls, it is actually almost something else, sort of a combo of an attenuated pyramid and an attenuated cone. Despite the omnidirectional symmetry of its inward tilt, it has an uneasy quality, which seems due in part to the lack of any vertical element in its composition. Not that the Cheesegrater steals its design thunder, but it does have that solid upright core going for it. If the shard had fewer facets, one could speculate that

it would seem more stable as a result: a bit more stalwartly pyramidal (though it's presumptuous to imply that this might be desirable). The dramatic treatment of the top with the facets eroding away is striking and pretty effective, but the proportions of the whole are such that this top condition can look like a bit of a mistake or some unfortunate damage: the gesture seems too small in proportion to the unremitting cone-ness of the shaft, if one may call it a shaft. All that said, though, these are rather minor cavils, for the project makes a convincing statement in general, to the advantage of the tilt as an expressive gesture; the point (no pun intended) is that with some adjustment to issues noted it might have been better yet.

Another tall building begs comparison, having also employed full height triangular facets with an inward tilt on ascent. But it's the differences between the Shard and One World Trade Center that are of note. I've made a bit of fun of the predictability of One's symmetrical faceting, but deference must be paid to certain of its merits (Fig.3.23.2). Weighted with unprecedented symbolic significance, it seems fair to say that the tower needed to be iconic but not too peculiar. Its alternating up and down facets achieve an upright profile from face approaches and a slight inward

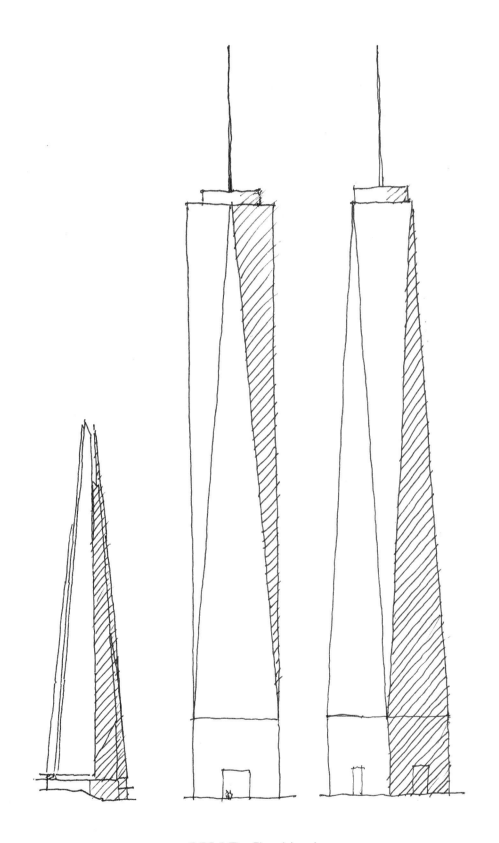

3.23.1 The Shard, London
3.23.2 One World Trade Center, NYC, @ 90° and 45°

tilt from 45° approaches, thus managing to incorporate both aspects in one shaft, should that be of any significance. The top and the base are disappointments, though, the former somehow unable to afford an appropriately cool pinnacle and the latter forced to become a raised concrete basement for ostensible security reasons, resulting in an awkward seam at the base of the triangles. In fact, the shaft's "closed system" of alternating triangles may have essentially made it impossible to achieve convincing terminating designs at either end.

Was it wrong for Libeskind's aping of the Statue of Liberty's asymmetrical profile to have been dismissed? Probably not. Was it too bad that a paired tower scheme such as Peterson Littenberg's was not seriously considered? Probably so. In that regard, with respect to paired towers, the absurd competition entry proposing open frameworks replicating the two volumes of the destroyed towers is not what is meant here. After all, the sole benefit of the 9/11 tragedy was to be rid of Yamasaki's clumsy volumetric profiles.

While we're on a roll with arguably defensible tall buildings with tilts, OMA's Beijing CCTV tower is indeed towering, but isn't really a tower, unless you deconstruct it into the bottom elbow, the top elbow, and the twin towers remaining (Fig. 3.24). If you reconstruct from the built figure as a remnant by extending the top elbow down and the bottom elbow up, you get a frustum of an attenuated pyramid, cut off on top at a slight angle and hollow in the middle. Every face tilts, except the top of the bottom elbow and the bottom of the top one. The combination of tilts crucially defuses mundanity from its play-puzzle formative diagram, and results in varied impressions from different angles, the most unsettling being the menacing maw-like quality

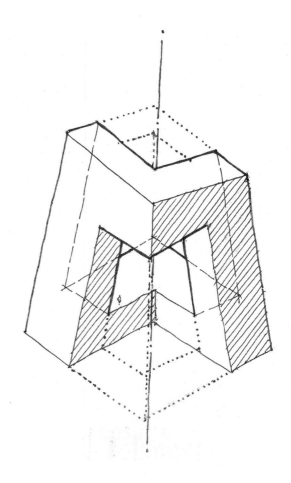

3.24 CCTV Headquarters, Beijing

of the big overhang. (Again with the maw thing. Maybe there's a thesis topic here.) As with most tall buildings there is no sense of human scale, but some compensation is offered by the pattern of expressed frame members, boldly defining structural realities instead of the imposition of a cosmetic pattern or grid. Ultimately the maw image is shared with one of a gateway, slightly recalling the Grande Arche de la Défense, but while the latter anchors (in its willful slightly skewed way) Paris' most compelling axis, the former (on the diagonal defined by the two elbows) relates in no particular way to Beijing's central area. The building just rears up amidst the urban chaos and roars its triumph.

In winding up this critique of buildings that

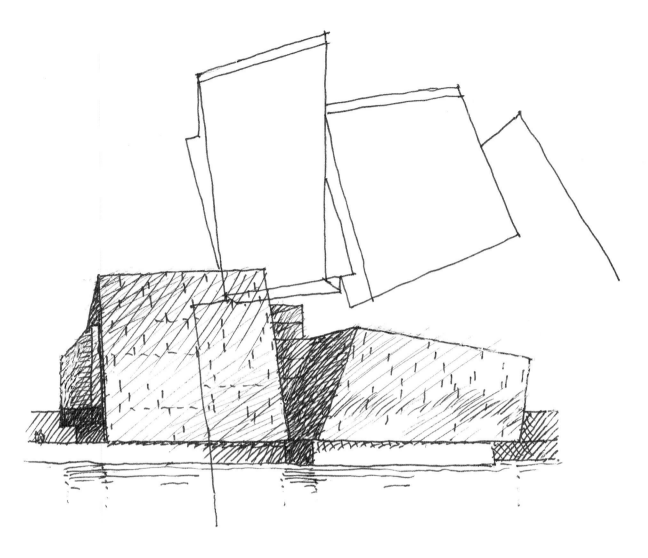

3.25 Harpa Concert Hall, Reykjavik

depend on tilting for their formative nature with at least some measure of success, something a bit more lower-rise again deserves attention. Reykjavik's Harpa Concert Hall and Conference Center, by Henning Larsen, is most often cited for Olafur Eliasson's unusual and colorful system of façade glazing elements, but its volumetric composition is the pertinent feature here (Fig. 3.25). The building seems at a glance to have no stable anchorage: all the planes of its two main volumes are tilting slightly this way, that way, or the other. But this very diversity of angled walls and planes actually adds up to a sense of mutual cohesion, and avoids the obvious and isolated hat tricks of leaning or bending or tipping or widening or narrowing. Notably, a number of secondary vertical surfaces do enhance a subtle sense of stability. Rather than resorting to a more obvious and singular "statement," this overall composition of adroitly related tilted surfaces among the major elements, in conjunction with secondary verticals, has achieved a convincing balance.

3c. Warping: A Twisted Tale

Simple convexity happens all the time in modernism: bullnosed stairwells; bowed façades or roofs; a million low-slope vaults stuck onto roadside boxes to help pretend that they are architecture. Concavity is not uncommon either, alongside convexity in the "piano curves" of Corbu and his emulators, or as inwardly bowed facades when the budget permits. These are not what is meant by "warping," being a rather inadequate general term for ways that specialized curvatures have burst to the fore in present century architecture, for good or ill.

Precedents

The spiral minaret of Samarra is a long-ago precedent for today's helical curvatures. In the past century, Wright's Guggenheim could also be cited, along with some other Wright works as well as some by Le Corbusier, Bruce Goff, and others (Fig. 3.26). Anticlastic or "doubly-curved" surfaces have made their most visible presence in architecture as hyperbolic paraboloids, in the forms of some dramatic roofs by the likes of Candela and Catalano, plus tensile structures, in common use to this day as shade or entry structures. They are part of the family of so called "ruled surfaces," certain of which have large parts to play in the projects that follow.

Straight up, With a Twist

There's a growing proliferation of high-rise buildings— almost all being abroad, to date—that are based on the helix, their surfaces forming double curvatures. The corkscrew

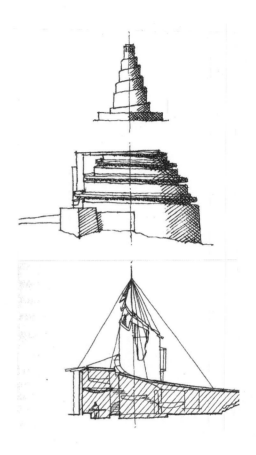

3.26 Great Minaret, Samarra, Iraq; Gordon Strong Automobile Objective, Frank Lloyd Wright (Unbuilt); Bavinger House, Bruce Goff, Norman, OK (Demolished)

forms of Diamond Tower, Jeddah, or Evolution Tower, Moscow, are but two examples (Fig. 3.27). Oddly, these evoke, at least for me, the Hellenistic sculpture of Laocoön and His Sons, figures in Greek mythology attacked by giant serpents sent by the gods. The towers' twisting forms, following each other in a chasing-tail succession that has no end, also seem a sort-of three-dimensional analog of the ouroboros--the snake that is eating its tail--said to suggest the eternal cycle birth and death. The type in all of its creepiness exists because it can: because

3.27 Diamond Tower, Jeddah, Saudi Arabia (Under Constr.) & Evolution Tower, Moscow, Flanked by Laocoön Group and Ouroboros

someone wanted to stand out from the crowd in the worst possible way and had the resources to do just that.

A subtype of such tall twisty buildings rotates only once or less in the course of ascent, thus not aspiring to the corkscrew image. SOM's Cayan Tower in Dubai rotates its vaguely open-book-shaped footprint 90 degrees clockwise from bottom to top (Fig. 3.28.1). One must admit that the resulting lack of repeating helical curvatures makes for a less disturbing aspect, though the impression that is made depends on orientation. With a vantage point parallel to one of the narrower faces at the base, the impression is a pronounced, stretched-looking x-shape that seems in kinetic motion and not in a good way. When facing a vertex at the base, a more graceful profile results that seems to expand and then contracts slightly on ascent. So the building has

its moments, but ultimately there are awkward aspects that cannot be avoided regardless of orientation, and these result directly from the utterly counterintuitive fundamental choice of twisting the thing on the way up.

ZHA's Generali Tower in Milan, a little more than half the height of the Cayan Tower, rotates its kite-shaped footprint only about half as much on ascent, largely straightening out in the top third or so (Fig. 3.28.2). The prominent grooves at opposite vertices emphasize the profile of the curvature, transitioning from a pronounced angle at the base to vertical at the top. The overall silhouette is less distorted and more vertical than the Cayan's, thereby imparting less of an impression that some sort of torqueing failure is underway. Aside from the grooves, the tower's surfaces are characteristically all but featureless, leaving a bit of an unsatisfied

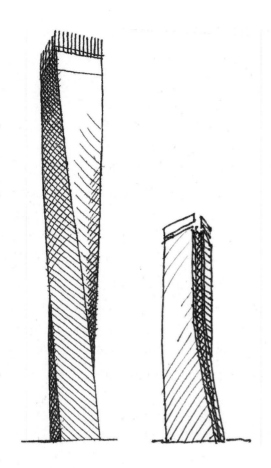

3.28.1 Cayan Tower, Dubai, UAE
3.28.2 Generali Tower, Milan

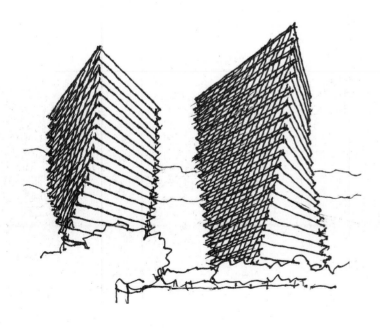

3.29 The Grove at Grand Bay, Miami

feeling: arguably an elegant entrée, but with no sides, and needing salt. The impressions noted thus far in the matter of twisting tall buildings would seem to have it that the less twist the better. And that said, a logical, if perhaps conservative, conclusion would have it that no twist at all might be best. Just a hypothesis—

High-rise towers being the exception—the extreme—when it comes to building proportion, what of the twist applied to lower rise projects? BIG offers the Grove at Grand Bay condos in Miami, two towers about a quarter the height of the Cayan (Fig. 3.29). And as with the Generali, the rotation of their rectangular footprints is 45 degrees from bottom to top, with the top third also straightening up. In fairness one assumes the result is what those involved wanted: something fundamentally new and different, a distinctive, rather *kinetic* looking address for the daring well-off. One must offer the impression that the somewhat stubbier proportions of these buildings can result in an unnerving impression that they have stopped rotating just momentarily—a brief photo op moment—before continuing to inexorably wind up (or is it wind down), the playing cards ending up in a neat stack, the gaps between them all squeezed out. From one vantage point an edge may give the illusion of verticality, only to be contradicted by other edges that radically slant. Another vantage point adds an impression that the mass is top-heavy, rendering the apparent composition even more kinetically unstable, as if it were the narrowing tip end of one of those corkscrews, its helix just begun, the point itself augured in.

Perhaps the Grove was too dull and predictable, for the architects moved on to Chelsea for "The XI" condo/hotel/office buildings, a pair of towers edging back up toward high rise in scale (Fig. 3.30). Each, on its requisite plinth, is a diabolical combination of two opposed elbows joined by two doubly curved surfaces. *And*, each elbow has one face that tilts out and one face that tilts sideways, each in the opposite direction of those on the other elbow. Got it? Think of the Veer towers at Vegas transitioned through the Twilight Zone with all three types of disorienting elements combined in the most varied possible ways, and differently on each exposure. The result variously appears to twist, tilt, or tip all at the same time. The metaphorical image of getting ready to twist into a stacked-up collapse recurs, and it may be that the tilting and tipping flat planes actually enhance the effect, suggestive of what an old-fashioned rectangular tower might look like if falling over in all directions at once. Reportedly this has been a much-awaited address for top-percenter cognoscenti, and since they live there (on occasion), they aren't obliged to deal with the vertigo that an overall exterior view offers. the project completes a set of Hudson River chess pieces, this tipsy king and queen next to Gehry's IAC negligee'd bishop next to Jean Nouvel's knight in crinkly armor.

Elevational High Jinks

No pun here, just a look at unwarranted high spirits in the application of a different variety of doubly curved geometry to some soon-to-not-be vertical surfaces. A precedent from the dark days of the '80's sets the stage: John Portman's Marriott Marquis in Atlanta is basically a pair of *conoids*, twinned about the centerline of

3.30 The XI, NYC. The IAC Building and 100 11th Avenue Condominium Tower Adjoin to North

the absurdly vertiginous atrium (Fig. 3.31). Evidently the term can mean a variety of things, but the geometric figure I remember from studying such matters long ago is a doubly curved surface generated by connecting a straight line with a curve. The Marquis in all its pregnancy is a rectangle at the top, but its long sides shortly begins to bow out, intersecting the inevitable plinth building below as an opposed pair of convex curves: two conoids.

SHoP's design for the US Embassy in Honduras offers a variant with two half conoids in a row, or to be more precise, a variation on that geometry with the arcs meeting the ground reformed as contraflexive curves (Fig. 3.32). (Or maybe just one of them actually does that; it's hard to tell. And that's a good thing, ambiguity being in short supply nowadays. Also of note, the scheme partakes effectively of "façade uncoupling" as well.) Whether the resulting slightly wavery elevations have some rationale in programmatic content or are simply another fabled shot at something different is not known at this writing. Publicity notes that these features evoke Honduras' mountainous terrain, though that seems a bit of a stretch. Well, as we architects know all too well, some such evocative imagery is often helpful in selling a bright idea, the abstractness of which might otherwise cause some wrinkled client brows.

BIG reappears to also offer a number of conoid applications. Their office building at the Philly Navy Yard features an inwardly bowed front that turns out to be a vertically oriented conoid surface as seen from the inside, when you are outside, so to speak (Fig. 3.33). The impression it makes, with rows of rectangular punched windows tilting at steadily varying angles, is inescapably one of something in the

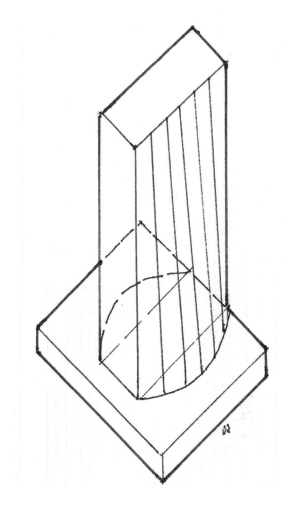

3.31 Atlanta Marriott Marquis

3.32 U.S. Embassy, Tegucigalpa, Honduras

66

process of going wrong—but what? The parapet is straight, so the wall is not falling over: that, at least, is good to know. The inward bow at grade offers nothing less than the impression that some massive force of suction on the interior is, well, sucking it in. And to what end, this surreal and tricky-to-construct set piece? One assertion on offer is that it responds to the metaphorical impact of the adjacent roundish parkscape; another that it curves like the bow of a battleship. Maybe so, though the connection is hardly readily apparent, the façade seeming a bit more immediately evocative of a collision with a battleship. But metaphors of collisions, while popular among architects, are a harder sell to the layperson.

The same geometry reappears, in an even harder-to-visualize form, at BIG's Isenberg School of Management addition at UMass Amherst, done with GoodyClancy (Fig. 3.34). Its falling dominos effect does provide the attention-getting centerpiece that an amorphous region of campus could use, though the relationship of the new to the existing is forced, the outermost of the massive dominos seeming about to crush the existing building with which they align. Perhaps, again, this is an unfair criticism for such a clever conceit, subtly validated by its dignified and costly copper cladding. As for the assertion that another conoid is to blame here, it is there: think of it as an upside down, backwards and cut-in-half version of the Navy's. And as opposed to the latter, here the seemingly quite deliberate impression is very much one of an assemblage in the process of falling over: of collapse. Which is yet another favored architectural metaphor but, again, probably not what was sold to the client.

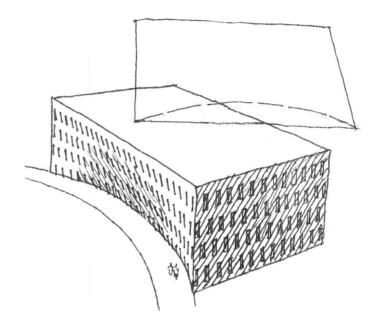

3.33 1200 Intrepid, Philadelphia Navy Yard

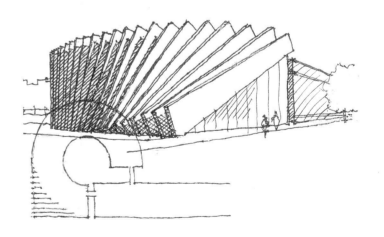

3.34 Isenberg School of Management Business Innovation Hub, University of Massachusetts, Amherst

Warpage You Can't Help but Like

Helsinki's Central Library (named "Oodi"), by ALA, finds itself hereabouts because it is based on another variation of a conoid surface (Fig. 3.35). But it's quite a variation: a convex curve extends way out and back along its substantial length, but instead of a straight line at the base, an arched vault swings over and into the building, with the whole complex curvature defined by spruce cladding. In contrast, the glass face of the big room on top is straight, but its parapet profile has its own pleasantly wavy curvature. In brief, the appeal of this project, redeeming its massive scale, arises significantly from its combination of curvatures, inside and out, warped and otherwise, in conjunction with straight edges and sharpish corners that lend authority but not rigidity. This matter of a combination of approaches, as opposed to a single bright idea, is important and may be

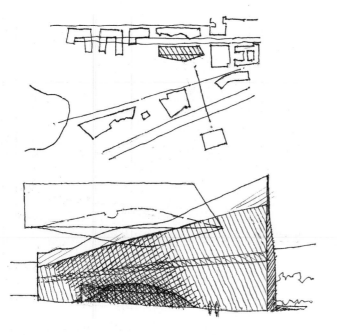

harped on some more elsewhere.

Another important topic that has not consumed much attention thus far is context, and the reason, frankly—in addition to the fact that peculiarity of form is the main subject at hand—is that these projects have often been self-important objects exhibiting limited responsiveness to context. But here, the library does yeoman service as a final puzzle piece in a series of defining elements, at the south end of what Aalto had proposed as massive plazas, tributes to his beloved splayed horizontals and greatly overextended at this urban scale. (Dare one assess him as a great architect but not so great an urbanist? That said, the district remains inadequately resolved to this day.) Regardless, would that more of these projects, so full of their peculiar themselves, had also served as well as urban spatial definers.

"Deformation": A Summary

As opposed to "fragmentation," which had clear progenitors, these typologies are more distinctly of the present century. Precedents from the recent and distant past are there to be found, but their links are largely indirect. These newly odd deal in different approaches to *distortion* as an overarching expressive means, via the self-describing modes of **stretching, tilting** and **warping**. To put it all in a simplistic nutshell, while the modes of fragmentation involved applications of pulling things apart and pushing them together, here a form may retain its cohesion but is variously subjected to pushing, pulling, and twisting, often for arbitrary dramatic effect: an architecture of bullying.

4 DEGRADATION: SHAPE CHANGED BY REMOVAL

Not meaning designs that are actually flat-out *degrading*, though in some cases this might indeed be considered the situation. Degradation here refers to—well, some synonyms could be *abatement, decomposition, degeneration*. It still sounds a bit negative, I guess, though it's true that not all projects employing the following approaches necessarily turn out to be the worse for wear. A distinction should be made, as with the approaches to deformation, that these don't involve "breakage," with the pieces now parts of a revised composition. Material does get removed in one way or another, but it doesn't stick around: only "traces" remain. The goal seems a "softening" of a work's morphology: a decrease in assertiveness and an increase in vagueness. A brave new world of the amorphous.

4a. Weakening: Edges Eroded

That title is a bit judgmental sounding, implying architecture that has lost its vim and vigor, literally or figuratively. The general idea is that a "normal" architectonic volume has lost some measure of clarity, for better or worse, though it's fair to note that under this umbrella there are occasional works that pull it off.

Precedents

These are harder to come by than in some other cases. As with "exfoliating," ruins, whether Roman or Romanesque, are loved by architects and could be a possibly subconscious forebear. Mannerism may also sort of count, with its visual trickery and unexpected elements undermining the norms of the Renaissance. In modern days the M word has been applied to the work of Robert Venturi and his ilk who favored ambiguity and contradiction. "The unexpected" characterizes some of the following, while others are more self-consistent. An overarching impression would be that something has been taken away—a plumb edge, a set of self-respecting corners, a restfully flat façade. And as opposed to earlier issues wherein the damaged goods remain as part of the changed ensemble, these are changes—removals—that are gone from the scene, leaving a "weakened" result.

Funny Edges

Or some call them corners, but the place where two sides come together, that's an edge. Well, the funny edges in question reveal a seeming weakness for taking nibbles—called "birdsmouth" cuts, a carpentry term—out of those oh, so continuous edges of high-rise buildings. We see it at Goettsch Partners' R&F Yingkai Square Tower in Guangzhou, where the nips or clips alternate side to side as they go up, lending a peculiarly wiggly impression. Manhattan's Hearst Tower, by Foster, goes full bore with the motif, the birdsmouths touching each other in succession up each edge and mating into the triangular "diagrid" patterns defining each building face. In both cases, "weakening" does seem an appropriate characterization (Fig. 4.1). The Hearst Tower in particular reminds one of a concertina, stretched to its limits, no dependable vertical edges left anywhere, the squeezebox looking ready to collapse back down momentarily.

I suppose there's no accounting for taste and some may like the look of those for some reason, but another case of funny edges defies a search for saving graces. Manhattan's 7 Bryant Park, by the Pei firm, applies concave carvings-out at a prominent exposure that converge, from the top and the bottom, to a squeaking singularity of ultimate convergence (Fig. 4.2). Awkward seems inadequate to describe this implosion, which proudly stands as the building's main statement, clearly an effort to do something that had never been done before, despite arguably good reasons for that having remained the case.

Funny Corners

For whatever reason, corners, as opposed to edges, have been less tempting as targets for the carving knives when those dull old rectilinear

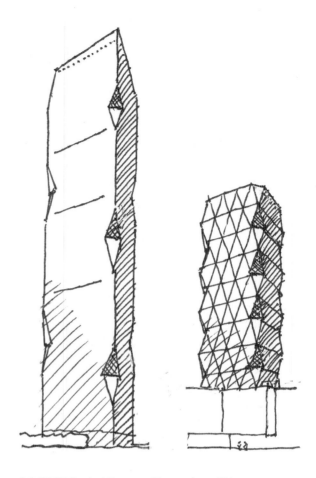

4.1 R&F Yingkai Square, Guangzhou, China; Hearst Tower, NYC

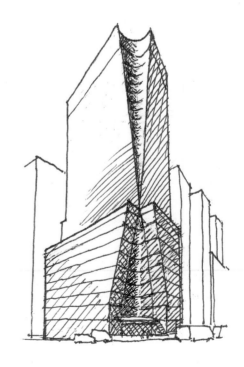

4.2 7 Bryant Park, NYC

4.3 Sheldon and Tracy Levy Student Learning Centre, Ryerson University, Toronto (Side and Front Elevations)

junctions just can't be borne any longer. The Student Learning Centre at Toronto's Ryerson University, by Snøhetta and Zeidler, will be our prize exhibit, though surely others are sprouting up at a brisk pace (Fig. 4.3). If there is a simplistic description of what's going on with the corners of this midrise block, it's one of chopping off diagonally opposite corners, leaving substantial triangular chamfers. Lest that appear too systematically obvious, further corner-related things are going on, primarily a "chamfer below a chamfer" to form a significant sloped soffit at the main entry. This eye-catching set of facets is treated to a bright blue glazed cladding treatment, a veritable sapphire being ground and polished into shape at building scale, or so one might assume was the architect's image as well as one having potential client appeal. Evidently the university wanted a signature statement and this does provide that, but the ultimate effect of all the buffing off of corners is to render it a bit clunkily neither fish nor fowl: with its perhaps unavoidably boxy proportions, and despite a resort to a slight tilting of some primary surfaces, the building volume is now neither hard nor soft but something a bit irresolutely in between, and tipsy looking in the bargain.

Funny Faces

Having scrutinized edges and corners, one notes that the surfaces that make them possible, a building's faces, have also been fooled around with in ways that can weaken a concept. But not necessarily, as with Robert Stern's Carpe Diem Tower in Paris and Heller Manus' 181 Fremont in San Francisco, both featuring "pleated" facades divided among slightly tilted facets (Fig. 4.4). (Pleating isn't really quite the correct term for this creased-and-bent morphology, but lacking a better one it will do.) The former is pleated on its opposite narrower elevations, with the latter, in very shallow relief, on all sides. Its expressed framework is the less elegant of the two, a chunky scale existing in response to the city's worrisome and, well, inevitable earthquake potential. In both cases the pleating does enliven the buildings' profiles and seems not to result in an appearance of "weakening," which intuitively one would think could indeed be a risk of such planar bends and breaks, vaguely suggestive that a destructive "crumpling" is getting underway. But hey, good for them, it seems to work in these cases, and bold 21st

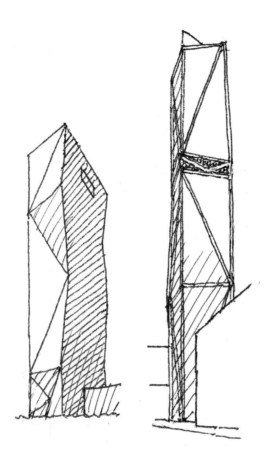

4.4 Tour Carpe Diem, La Défense, Paris; 181 Fremont, San Francisco

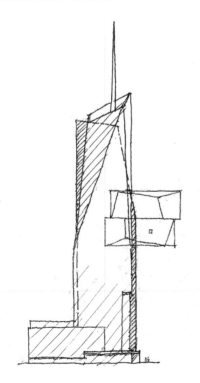

4.5 Bank of America Tower, NYC

century formative innovations that seem to work do deserve notice amidst all those that don't so much.

As for a lower-rise version, Krueck & Sexton's FBI office building in Florida, first met earlier in the context of detached facades, also features some pleated treatment (Fig. 2.20). The inconspicuous junctures of its facets give the impression of a single surface that has been creased a bit, with a rather elegant result that, if anything, gives added perceived strength to the façade. So on the strength of these few projects, a shallow pleating of vertical faces emerges relatively unscathed in our hunt for the questionably weakeningly peculiar. And not surprisingly, for they're really a bit out of place here, such creasing involving no "removal of material": since the enclosing fabric remains intact, there is, as it turns out, no conclusive sense of "weakening"

. . .

The high-rise façades of Cook + Fox's Bank of America Tower in Manhattan sport neither chamfers nor pleats, but very elongated triangular or trapezoidal facets (Fig. 4.5). They facilitate a pretty convincing expression of a volume's gradual diminution with height: in effect, a modern movement version of the setback treatments exemplified by the Empire State and Chrysler Buildings. The unassertive flatness of these surfaces contrasts dramatically with the awkward concavity of similarly attenuated facets at 7 Bryant Park nearby. These stretched out facets recall some of the "tilting" cases, such as the Shard and One World Trade Center, but a distinction is clear, for the latter involve full-height applications of tilting surface as opposed to partial height facets. One is obliged to note that BOA's base condition is disappointing, and that a design feature expressive of shear—the volume appearing to have split down the middle with the two halves bypassing slightly—offers a couple of arguably awkward conditions, but these issues don't detract markedly from the overall impression. Even the pinnacle, which simply extends from the middle of one of the two (visually) canted roofs, is fairly convincing, certainly more so than some attempts to blend a skinny and nonfunctional extension with the top of a corner instead. (Such was the case with the intermediate "wind turbine farm" version of One WTC, a particularly awkward step in the gradual morphing of that building design from one architect's daringly odd concept to another's mighty unchallenging reality.) And the BOA Tower again bears comparison with the Shard, to the advantage of the former (their very different contextual settings aside). True vertical faces of the former extend fully to the top, affording the sense of anchorage that one misses in the London project, wherein all facades, notably expressed as freestanding planes that further subtly undermine a sense of stability, converge slightly from the vertical.

Facets All Over

So "faceting and pleating," at least within the bounds of well-considered design such as noted above, have largely acquitted themselves with honor as enhancements of buildings' upright faces. But a confluence of all three of these funny things that get done to self-respecting buildings is another story. Consider Nouvel's Hekla Tower for Paris (Fig. 4.6). Indeed, they're all there: triangular cut off corners, edges banged into by randomized confluences (though birdsmouth bites seem not to have been taken), facades fragmented into a seemingly

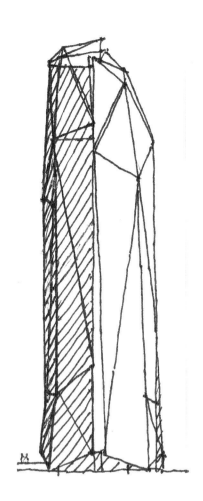

4.6 Hekla Tower, La Défense, Paris

chaotic montage of variously proportioned and angled triangular facets. The architect is said to have imagined its silhouette as a "crystal but in a compact form," whatever that may mean, though it's true that the ever-popular faceted crystal imagery has clearly been an influence. (And one can't help but recall "The Dark Crystal," a puppet-animated film wherein the eponymous object certainly bore some resemblance to Hekla. One draws the line, though, at also referencing the movie's "shard" with respect to London's Shard—)

The Ryerson University project gave us a foretaste of the ultimate version of such faceting and chamfering galore. While the

Hekla Tower inevitably retains its identity as a tower, despite evident efforts to make it look like an inscrutable something else, lower rise buildings fully reveal the consequences when faceting truly takes over as an unconstrained formative cancer. Minneapolis' U.S. Bank Stadium by HKS offers an entry in the popular effort to make a huge indoor stadium look like something unnameable, and the incorporation of aspects of human scale has evidently been abandoned as hopelessly old-fashioned in favor of desirably jaw-dropping brobdingnagian oddity (Fig. 4.7.1). The oddity of choice in this case is a selection of enormous triangular and trapezoidal facets, some metal, some glass, stuck together to form much of the exterior. It must be admitted that pointy things can potentially evoke a desirably dynamic quality, but here, excepting the stuck-on prow, they just get in each other's way.

Atlanta's Mercedes-Benz Stadium by HOK and others apparently hoped to bring some more consistently applied formative order to another enclosed stadium, despite the challenge that great big triangular facets were again, unaccountably, thought to be a good cladding theme for that purpose (Fig. 4.7.2). While the sky opening operates, ingeniously enough, like a camera iris, the bright idea of adopting that sequentially folding-in look for the whole exterior—all triangles all the time, without a horizontal edge to be found—succeeds mainly in looking as if these facades may also momentarily be—zzzzzzip—stacked together in the middle somehow.

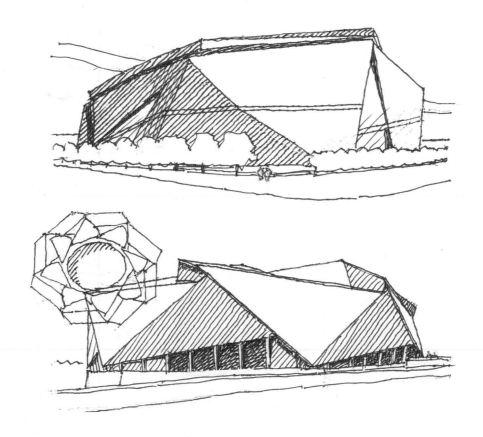

4.7.1 U.S. Bank Stadium, Minneapolis
4.7.2 Mercedes-Benz Stadium, Atlanta

. . .

Two earlier projects by OMA sum up the bad and the good of this facets-gone-feral approach. The Seattle Central Library, its interiors praised by some, offers a baffling concatenation of exterior facets to its urban setting (Fig. 4.8.1). Ostensibly the direct outcome of a nightmare Christmas package wrapping effort, or, alternatively, a sort of shrink-wrapping of the complicated stack of interior elements, the logic of the result does not redeem its looming, brooding peculiarities, among them several super-scalene triangles that seem diabolically attached at their super-pointy ends, ready at any moment to swing down on that hinge with a mighty crash. A belt of vertically oriented faces midway up affords the composition's only remnant of the orthogonal.

Turning to the firm's Casa de Musica in Porto, a not dissimilar set of play pieces comes together more felicitously (Fig. 4.8.2). A belt of vertical surfaces again girdles the single volume, bounded here by various polygonal facets extending down as roof surfaces and up as steeply sloping soffits. The site, an island of public open space surrounded by streets, renders this version of "building as crystal" a convincing choice. The lack of anomalous outrigging points or gapped-open joints reinforces the affirmation of the scheme, and windows are artfully handled so as never to seem an unfortunate interruption or puncture. The overall impression is one of a volume that is all facets, their proportions and junctions influenced by the interior accommodations but without the literal-minded eccentricity of the Seattle project, and with the "belt" effectively establishing a sense of stability. The fact that chamfered corners, as at the Toronto project,

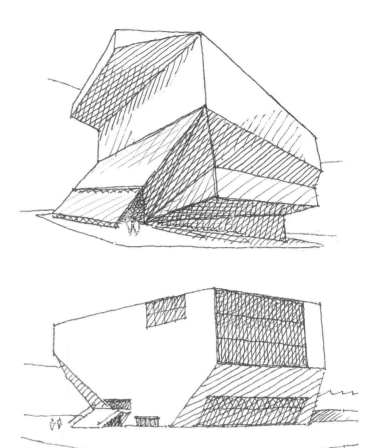

4.8.1 Seattle Central Library
4.8.2 Casa da Música, Porto, Portugal

were not resorted to also benefits the result. So facets (or pleats) don't necessarily weaken a project: if done well they can strengthen it, although this does seem a challenge.

Funny Innies

Sometimes such weakenings get more aggressive, appearing as peculiar breaches in a building's surface. It should be said at the outset that "cutout" conditions—entries, colonnades, niches, notches, just plain assorted odd-looking windows—are architecturally ubiquitous and not our concern here. We are thinking of biomorphic shreds, carvings, excisions. The big ovaloid thing that is Vegas' T-Mobile Arena, by Populous (ah, yet another arena: their odd nature as buildings does seem to attract correspondingly odd architectural treatments nowadays) features a couple of concentric "detached" façade elements—recalling that trope of exfoliation—one of which features some big irregular tears or rips (Fig. 4.9). They look a bit like a face: frowning brow, squinting eye, grimacing mouth. True, from a different angle it's a little more friendly looking, and the whole thing was surely meant to be bold but not to encourage flat-out pareidolia, at least so one hopes. They still look like rips and tears, though.

Holl designed a remarkable museum complex for Tianjin, China—now on hold for quite a while; we'll hope not forever—of which the formative concept was to carve biomorphic shapes out of one museum and set them down next door to become the other one (an oversimplification but not a completely inaccurate one). The irregular curved openings, with glazing deeply recessed from the building's faces, were confidently artful in their strangeness (Fig. 4.10.1). One sees the memory of those shapes in the architect's

Hunters Point Library for Queens, but now they are glazed nearly flush with the building face, and there is scant correspondence of the interior volumes with their outlines, the shapes thereby becoming more fully a two-dimensional, abstract, minimalist composition at a very large scale (Fig. 4.10.2). From the entry side, there is even a bit of pareidolia potential. From the river side, the oddness and bigness of the shapes give the ultimately boxy shape of the building a desirable presence, not a face or anything recognizable but intriguing in its big scale and a focus for the lineup of uninteresting skyscrapers adjoining. So these thin cutouts aren't innies per se, but a brave exercise in surficial configuration.

Dallas' Perot Museum of Nature and Science by Morphosis, another concrete box, does something more jagged and violent along these lines and thus more in character with the work of that firm (Fig. 4.11). One whole edge is broken open and stove-in, with the slanting glass box housing an escalator looking not so much like the cause of the damage as a band aid to hold the breakage in place. While the library

4.9 T-Mobile Arena, Las Vegas

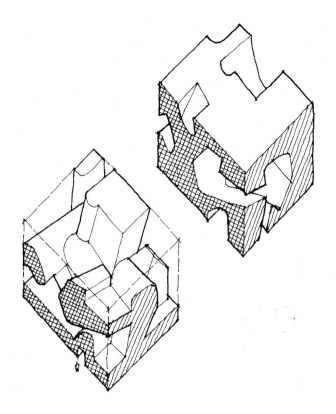

4.10.1 Tianjin, China Ecocity Ecology and Planning Museums (Concept)

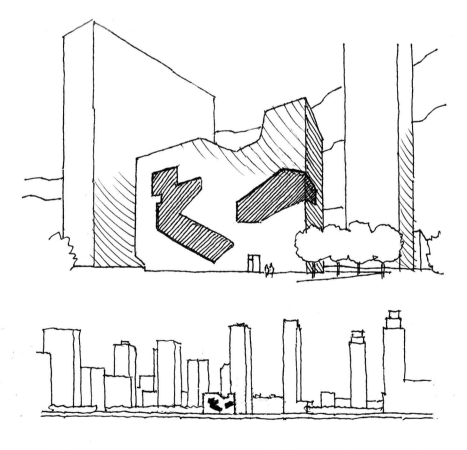

4.10.2 Hunter's Point Community Library, NYC (Near and Distant Views)

is painted silver for a sleek and monolithic impression, the museum's exterior features not pleats or wrinkles but bent-out horizontal cuts, kind of wince-inducing, that are said to evoke geological strata. The box's base is surrounded in part by shrapnel as if cast of by the apocalyptic event the composition evokes. The place is popular as a kid's museum, with exhibits by others which circulate well on the interior, but one wonders what visitors really think of the banged-up box that is the container. The cuts remind us of the rucked-up carpet image that pertained to stratifying as compression: here they increase from the top down, as if the lower reaches were indeed being subject to some sort of unfortunate progressive delamination, due to damp rising from the basement or some such.

Bless 'em, I do like a lot of Morphosis' work, but the firm provides yet another pertinent example of gratuitous inniness (actually outiness in this case), at Manhattan's 41 Cooper Square: a normal rectangular solid trying its best to look like something else (Fig. 4.12). As opposed to stove-in, its façade-scrim appears to have blown open from the inside on the evidence of assorted outward-bent rips and gaps. Which is enough to make the point for purposes of this subhead, though it bears noting that the project also offers the appearance (and sometimes the reality) of being encapsulated by scrims, variously disconnected outboard of its facades—sometimes "violently" in this case—another feature pertinent to the earlier discussion of "facade uncoupling."

Ultimate Innies

There's a sort of ultimate version of these assorted ways of cutting or puncturing things, which can sometimes run the risk of weakening

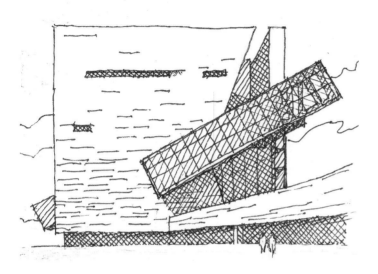

4.11 Perot Museum of Nature and Science, Dallas

4.12 41 Cooper Square, NYC

78

a building's "basic idea": namely, the through-passing hole. Holes that look at the sky, such as the courtyard of D.C.'s Hirshhorn Museum or in the low-rise part of Manhattan's Lever House, don't attract our attention as notably peculiar, the courtyard building being a ubiquitous archetype, but it's a different story when it's a horizontal hole in a vertical building. An obvious historical precedent is the gate, the monumental gates of Rome or China's moon gates among many examples. It takes raising the floor of that opening to change the whole idea: to isolate the hole and turn the building into an upright torus, topologically speaking. Back in the '80's it was biggish news when Dallas' Chase Tower, by SOM, burst upon the postmodern scene with a hole through its upper reaches. Paris' Grande Arche de la Défense, also from those days, is *mostly* hole.

In the 21ˢᵗ Century, China seems the current headquarters for punctured buildings (Fig. 4.13). The Gate of the Orient in Jiangsu returns to the gate precedent, its inverted U profile a hugely attenuated version, while the Sheraton Huzhou's upright profile is a truer torus, and Guangzhou Circle features a hole concentric with its own round profile. Beijing's Sunrise Kempinski Hotel adds its own variation on the theme. It's only fair to ask whether these "moon gate" buildings are problematic or not: odd they are and intentionally so, but not in an aggressively off-putting way. Let's face it, they're kind of charming; completely lacking in human scale, but that's sort of the idea. The notion of having your hotel room or office in something that looks a bit like a thrill ride is part of the fun. With that bold assertion, before leaving China a momentary recall of the CCTV Headquarters seems called for, regarding the ambiguity of its form: does it define a hole as well—we did wonder if it might be perceivable as sort of a gateway—or is it too much of a zigzag to do enough real defining?

ZHA is rapidly becoming the chieftain of buildings with big holes in them. Sunrise Tower in Kuala Lumpur, Hotel Morpheus in Macau, the Opus in Dubai: who knows where this trend will lead (Fig. 4.14). Some feature multiple holes, some are not yet built as of this writing. All appear to be much about providing Instagram and selfie moments for the very well off who can afford to stay in their hotels or

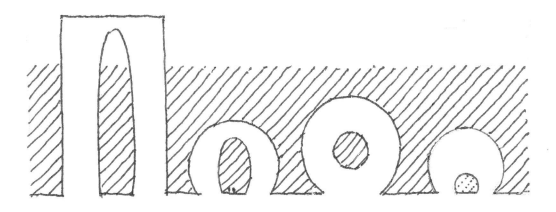

4.13 Gate of the Orient, Jiangsu; Sheraton Huzhou; Guangzhou Circle; Sunrise Kempinski Hotel, Beijing

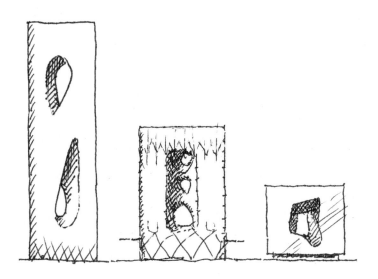

4.14 Sunrise Hotel, Kuala Lumpur; Hotel Morpheus, Macau; The Opus, Dubai

Morphosis' Emerson College in LA (sort of), that long ago Miami condo by Arquitectonica (Fig. 4.15). Something to ponder: whomever has the office or the apartment or whatever facing the hole gets to look into someone else's. It's a trendy upscale version of a light well, sideways, focusing outward in midair with a deliberate disconnect from the site context. Are such buildings with holes symptomatic of conceptual "weakening"? Inevitably that comes down to a matter of opinion as do many of the cases in this chapter, but one opinion would hold that, in some of these examples, the contrast of rectilinear solidity with melting orifices represents simply too wide a gap between morphological approaches: there is a mutual contrast which doesn't act to the advantage of either.

Erosion as a Literal Motif

lease their offices, the buildings' natures having entailed astronomical construction costs. But authoritarian regimes wishing to be on point with such expensive fads can be, no problem. The exterior exoskeletons of some, in conjunction with the biomorphic, "melting" quality of the orifices, summon up a subliminally sinister vibe of a trussed-up building gasping to be released.

Well, the more you look, they're all over: the Domino developments by SHoP in Brooklyn,

Continuing to think in terms of a sequence, one could visualize two different endpoints to this process of cutting, bending, or removing elements or pieces or parts from an "initiating architectonic volume." Boring a hole would be the macro version—one big chunk of something gone—while the other extreme might be the removal of many small increments (or ultimately, infinitesimally small increments,

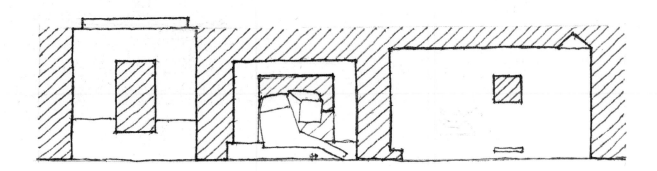

4.15 325 Kent, NYC; Emerson Los Angeles; Atlantis on Brickell, Miami

as if by "sandblasting," which turns out to be a lead-in to the next chapter). But in terms of increments that are legible, pixelization is the inevitable buzzword, for the moment at least. Dare I note that a precedent appeared in the '80's in the form of NYC's Trump Tower, its clumsy, bustle-like base incrementally pixilating its way up to its pleated tower. Nowadays the approach is more strikingly visualized by Ole Scheeren's King Power MahaNakhon resdential tower in Bangkok (Fig. 4.16). The concept is obvious enough, with an irregularly carved helical path winding its way up a tall glass box, summoning the unnerving impression of an eating-away of the glass skin and the "flesh" beneath by this invasive snake. Or to be less zoomorphic about it, a more general impression of a building in the process of suffering a disastrous deconstruction: surely it's about to collapse, in a heap of pixels. That image places this "erosive image" firmly in the lineage of leitmotifs about weakening.

Decades ago, Albania was the one European country you couldn't visit, Stalinist and bleak, its borders closed. I once shared a day-long rail trip to Istanbul with an Albanian salesman who eventually confessed that he had *escaped* from Albania. Who knew we would now see up-to-the-faddish-moment high-rises in Tirana, such as MVRDV's "Downtown One" (Fig. 4.17). Up the middle of this straightforward gridded box building, pixels pop in and out, a perfectly squared fruit rotting from the inside. And in another as yet unbuilt variation on this theme by the architect, the proposed "Milestone" tower in Esslingen, Germany, the erosion goes all the way through, a ragged-edged version of boring a hole through the middle. Thus a case where each endpoint of the innie morphological sequence serves the other.

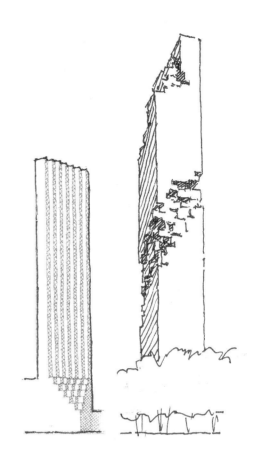

4.16 Trump Tower, NYC; King Power MahaNakhon, Bangkok

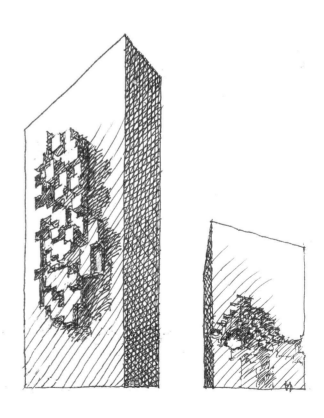

4.17 Downtown One, Tirana, Albania; Milestone Tower, Esslingen, Germany

81

4b. Smoothing: Edges Gone

The implications and results of "smoothing" in architectural expression are both among the most strikingly visible and potentially the most troubling among the "manifestations of the peculiar" in 21st century architecture. It's important to clarify at this point that smoothing refers not only to surfaces, often rendered in singularly uninterrupted treatments—"the rough places plain"—but to edges as well, buffed, eased and polished and thereby made edges no longer.

Precedents

Large curvatures in architecture date way back in the form of masonry vaults and domes, with more complex contraflexive curves appearing in Baroque times. The early 20th century finds the more irregular expressionist curves of Mendelsohn's Einstein Tower or Gaudi's Casa Mila. Le Corbusier's Notre Dame du Haut would seem to count as expressionist or perhaps neo-expressionist, as would Saarinen's TWA Flight Center at JFK. Kiesler's never-built "endless house" seems almost an exercise in handbuilt ceramic shapes, expressionist indeed with its bulbous forms morphing one into another. Hyperbolic paraboloid surfaces began appearing mid-century last—they appear in the discussion on "warping"—while inflatable structures are defined by domical curvatures of one degree or another. So it's clear that architecture up to the present century hardly lacked for smooth and often irregularly defined convexities and concavities. But the point for this discussion is that some more recent work has drilled down to focus on these attributes as virtually a *sole* means of expression.

As a sort of prequel, Foster + Partners were responsible in the earliest years of this century for a couple of startling and well-known London projects: 30 St. Mary Axe ("The Gherkin") and the London City Hall (Fig. 4.18). The former, essentially a prolate spheroid, is completely symmetrical, while the latter, stubbier form leans very distinctly away from the waterfront, as if blown over by some strong winds or, perhaps, having been left out in the sun too long. Both are notably sleek and smooth looking, perhaps having helped set the stage for more radical manifestations of smoothing to come.

Coop Himmelb(l)au's Work as Formative Mediator

The Viennese firm has done a far-ranging variety of work, much of it of the "watch out-it's sharp" variety. But there is a sequence, not necessarily chronological, that reveals the increasing involvement of large curvatures amongst the edginess, comprising another sort of

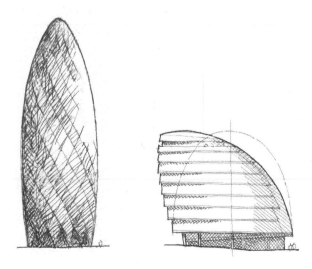

4.18 30 Saint Mary Axe, London; City Hall, London

82

prequel. Their BMW Welt complex in Munich is basically a three-layer sandwich, its multi-angled base supporting long planes of angled glazing (Fig. 4.19.1). But the big cantilevered cap offers a distinctively different aspect in the serpentine curvatures of its soffit, plus another appearance of curvature prominently showing up in the unconvincing hyperboloid volume that spins up to (or down out of?) this big cap. That element seems intended to provide a root or point of origin for the hovering roof, but is an awkward fit for that purpose, and its triangular "scales" give the impression of popping off due to the "torque stresses" involved, leaving a jagged border at the transition from metal to glass which does the scheme no favors. These elements of curvature, while bold and important parts of the composition, are not integral parts, and no one would characterize the project as having "smoothness."

Their Musée de Confluences in Lyon is an assembly of crimped and cut flat surfaces of shiny cladding and glass that call up the image of a crocodile having emerged from the river to chomp its way toward downtown (Fig. 4.19.2). But curvatures are again showing up: several concave and convex conditions coexist uncomfortably with the otherwise crisp corner and edge conditions. More to the point, the longitudinal skyline of the overall building approximates a long downward curve toward the two bladelike ends. So while even more aggressive than the earlier Munich project, it has this ghost of overarching curvature.

Their International Conference Center in Dalian, China presents a far smoother overall form, with a broad, flattened carapace like a streamlined turtle or an alien spacecraft (Fig. 4.19.3). Along the side flanks of the massive structure, the tables have been turned regarding the emergence of curvature amongst hard edges, for here the latter seem to be all but engulfed. But some do remain, resulting in some awkward junctions with smoothly modulating surfaces. In a notable innovation, apparently in an attempt to incorporate transparent openings as inconspicuously as possible, layers of many thinly profiled openings appear as if weaknesses in the layered or scaled epidermis that have sagged and gapped open, these thin serried gaps recalling some "blobitecture" experiments in the '90's by the Greg Lynn office. Ultimately the building exhibits the difficulties of a half-way blending of crisp edges with smoothly curved surfaces, pointing to the logical next step: architecture that is more completely defined by continuous curvature, with corresponding positive and negative ramifications.

River Tumbled

Buildings defined volumetrically by true continuity of curvature: these are projects from which straight edges have been banned: expunged, as if hopelessly retardataire. Studies have been bandied about to the effect that we prefer curves in our built environment because they signal a lack of threat, while objects with sharp elements activate the amygdala, the part of the brain that processes fear. Could be, but other studies have concluded that this "threat association hypothesis" can't fully explain the appeal of curvature as opposed to straight line imagery. It's easy to get bogged down in competing theories and experiments, and, indeed, someone has to do it, and we're glad that a smidgen of evidence basis for evidence-based design is beginning to be eked out. But this is not a scholarly piece: it is an "informed

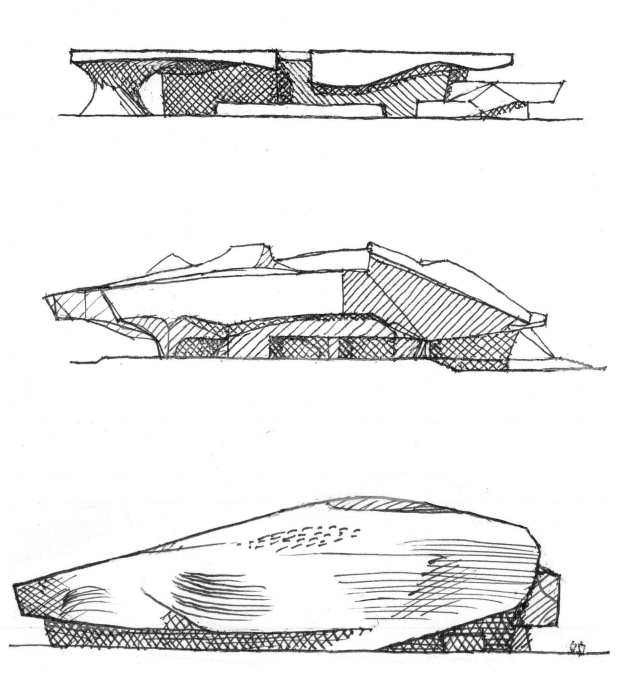

4.19.1 BMW Welt, Munich, Germany
4.19.2 Musée des Confluences, Lyon, France
4.19.3 Dalian International Conference Center, Dalian, China

opinion" piece, based primarily on a fair amount of background in designing and experiencing architecture.

The term "river tumbled" should pretty clearly evoke the sort of form definition referenced: irregular shapes without edges, and a smooth continuity of exterior surface throughout. For reasons one might speculate upon—authoritarian nations with unlimited money at the centers of power, perhaps?—expensive, inefficient and difficult-to-engineer buildings of this description have a way of showing up in places like China and Saudi Arabia. Somewhat less so in the west, so far. The King Abdulaziz Center for World Culture in Dhahran, called "Ithra," is a sort of shopping mall of culture with museums, libraries, exhibit halls, theaters (Fig. 4.20). Snøhetta's conceit is that the several distinct volumes actually appear more wind-worn than river tumbled, with hints remaining that they were once defined by distinct straight edges. A stack-o-stones image is deliberate and referred to as such by the architects. The composition evokes the sort of small totem of stones a youngster might stack together, and as such has a scaleless quality that fails to manifest its very-large-scale reality. Is it problematical in its smoothness? The arrangement is artful enough and admittedly suits its immediate context, a tailored region of the largely uninhabitable desert that is the Arabian Peninsula inboard of the coast. The complex has the distinction, perhaps dubious, of being sited in the same place as the first Saudi-discovered oilfield, which ultimately will have rendered its existence possible. Windows are an inherent design problem when all surfaces are smooth irregular curvatures: here a few wide stripes criss-crossing the one upended "stone" incorporate glazed openings and recall geomorphological intrusions—known to geologists as dykes—of a different and darker rock.

The project slightly recalls ZHA's earlier Guangzhou Opera House, its two volumes multifaceted with eased edges, and said by

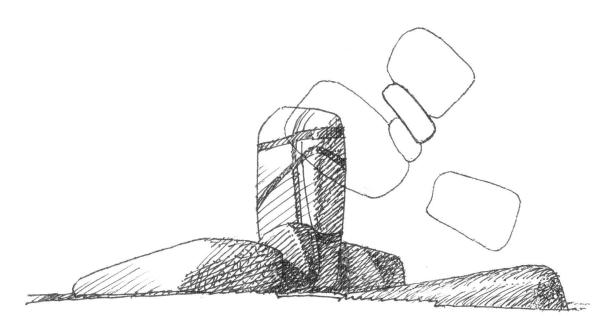

4.20 King Abdulaziz Center for World Culture, Dhahran, Saudi Arabia

the architect to have been "shaped to resemble pebbles in the Pearl River" (Fig. 4.21). The problem of fenestration is less felicitously resolved in this case with its wrappings of big, oddly shaped glass areas. The composition seems clunky from some angles, while a ubiquitous money shot presents a signal aggressiveness, as of two abstract sharks thrusting forward with teeth bared (maws, yet again). The project is an early manifestation of the approach, its facets and edges still quite distinct as opposed to the more complete smoothings-out of later works.

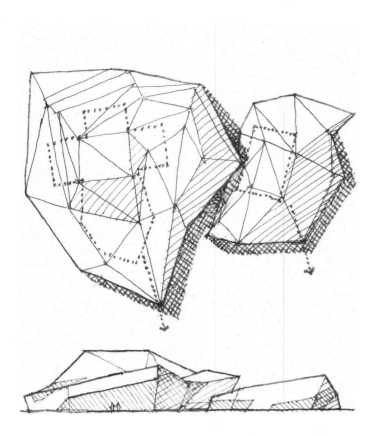

4.21 Guangzhou Opera House, Guangzhou, China

River Tumbled to a Fare-Thee-Well

Much of the Hadid office's later work inevitably becomes the centerpiece of a discussion of "ultimate smoothness" in architectural expression. Beijing's Wangjing SOHO office complex departs completely from even the slightest ghosts of edges, its three forms completely smoothed into varying concavo-convex volumes (Fig. 4.22). They all emerge at their widest extents at the ground plane as if but topmost extensions of a geomorphological structure, like Australia's Ayers Rock. Not featureless, but almost—their irregular spacings of horizontal banding faintly recalling that image of geological dykes—they have a somewhat wet-and-slippery quality, which actually struck me before reading that they were "partially inspired by the anatomy of koi fish." Ultimately the total absence of a sense of focus, entry or (dare I say it) the bracing presence of an edge, anywhere—renders these looming water-balloony things just slightly disturbing. From the standpoint of their immediate urban context, they sit at the focus of an anomalously beaux-arty urban

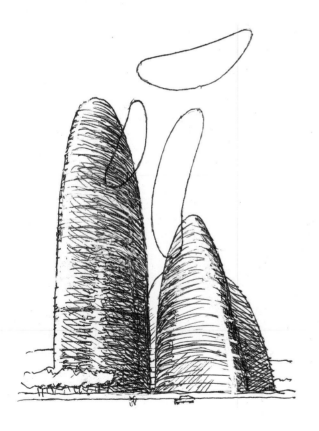

4.22 Wangjing SOHO Complex, Beijing

86

composition, backed by a semicircular ring road and terminating a substantial axial open space. The project makes no gestures to the structure of this setting, treating it as a deferential plinth for the display of a freestanding work of sculpture, which it rather self-importantly seems to regard itself to be.

Stretched

"Smoothing" can be seen as the result of several different imagined but conceptually powerful processes. Erosion—the gradual subtraction implicit in river tumbling or grains of sand in the wind—defines the immediately preceding projects. But a quite different smoothing outcome arises from the "deformative" act of pulling or stretching apart. A bold but tentative shot at this approach appears in the much-publicized Selfridges store by Future Systems in Birmingham, U.K., and Asymptote's Yas Hotel in Abu Dhabi: in both cases, a sort of blanket appears thrown over more conventional forms and pulled or stretched into place (Fig. 4.23). Thus, to one degree or another, these are a sort of hybrid of a solid armature and a partial and morphable—stretchable—outer scrim.

ZHA's One Thousand Museum, not a museum but a condominium tower in Miami, adopts a related but evolved approach, the scrim now a linear webwork. Stretched the full height, it seems to laterally compress the stack of floor plates like a sort of girdle, and indeed this network serves significant structural functions. (Fig. 4.24). The interstices it defines offer a notably insectile impression: the thing might bite if you're not careful. The building slightly recalls some aspects of Gaudi's Basilica de la Sagrada Familia, though the latter is characterized more by vegetative- or grotto-like

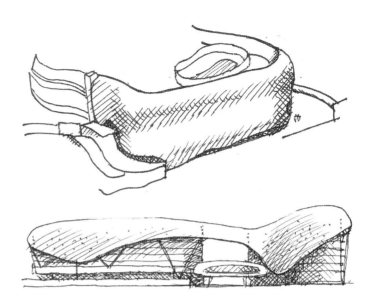

4.23 Selfridges Building, Birmingham, UK; Yas Hotel, Abu Dhabi, UAE

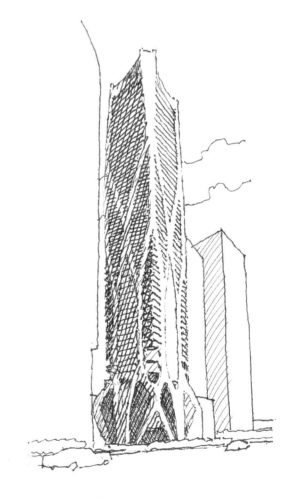

4.24 One Thousand Museum, Miami

imagery, its forces descending to grade rather than twisting taut and ready to snap.

Hadid's competition-winning version of the Japan National Stadium, which went on to be sorely truncated and eventually unselected, is sort of an apotheosis of this stretching image (Fig. 4.25). Compared to the condo tower, the unique formative nature of a stadium permits a more consistently realized figure-ground duality, here a stretchy looking linear network that contains a closest-packing infill of biomorphic lenses. The way the network appears pulled taut over its pregnant centerpiece—the ghost volume of the stadium bowl—has evolved from the closed forms of a project like Wangjing SOHO into one stretched beyond a breaking point, the overall domical covering pulled apart into strands, like deconstructing bubble-gum. And beyond this abstract but evocative imagery, the project recalls nothing so much as a horseshoe crab without the pointy things on its carapace; something from the shore, smoothed and taut but a bit menacingly alive.

Pushmi-Pullyu

A bubble-gum-like membrane again appears prominently in MAD Architects' Harbin Opera House, but it embodies a more complex, less axial imagery of stretching (Fig. 4.26). Two dominant volumes center on vaguely disturbing translucent elements, complex knobs with rugged surfaces in need of a shave. These elements variously seem solid and unmoving outgrowths of the overall plinth, or as if a bit molten, pushing up and out against their smooth and malleable white overcoat. That contrasting element has been pushed around and squeezed in to wrap the anchorages. (Or have the latter grown up and out? Or both?) Regardless, the white integument has sheared open into gaps, evoking tensile failures. And dare one note there seems something just a tad, well, genital about the formative ensemble; presumably unintended but a bit unnerving.

The Heydar Aliyev Center in Baku, yet another ZHA work, is a more direct evocation of "pushes and pulls" that alternate in their effects. (Fig. 4.27). Unlike any of the preceding

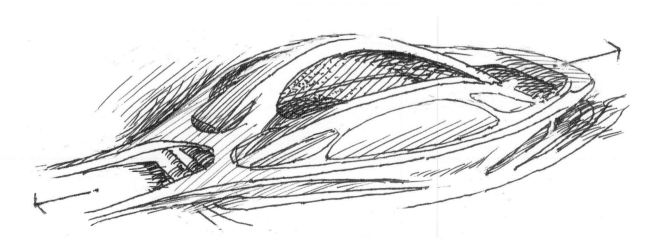

4.25 Japan National Stadium (Initial Design)

projects that exemplify smoothing in one way or another, there is no fundamental or initiating volume here: this flamboyant homage to a cult-centric autocrat is a planar surface—plasticine rolled flat—that has been variously pushed, pulled, stretched, shoved (and cut a bit as well) to achieve a result that is not remotely axial or central but something that manages to avoid either. It's hard to escape the impression that Heydar is keeping one or another eye on you, brows lifted high in autocratic suspicion. And from the right angle, the sets of serried crooked descents to the datum plane again look almost insectile, as if the whole inscrutable thing might spring up at a moment's notice. The project, pristine and white inside and out, ceilings blending to walls and walls to floors, is said to be expertly crafted, but the human visitor appears lost in such an interior, or even, dare one postulate, an unnecessary or unwanted feature.

4.26 Harbin Opera House, China

Melted

Several of the preceding projects could readily evoke a sense of "deformation by overheating" as much as by a more corporeal potter's work image. The Stadium's bubblegum may have warmed up in proportion to its axial stress and delaminated thereby; maybe the Harbin's inflows got hot and subsided; the Aliyev perhaps similarly sagged between its pulled-up places. The holes in Figure 4.14 have a bit of a melted look. But those are "alternative" imagined forces.

At least one project looks for all the world like it was put out in the noonday sun and left there too long with catastrophic results: Gehry's Lou Ruvo Center for Brain Health in Las Vegas (Fig. 4.28). The architect famously works with

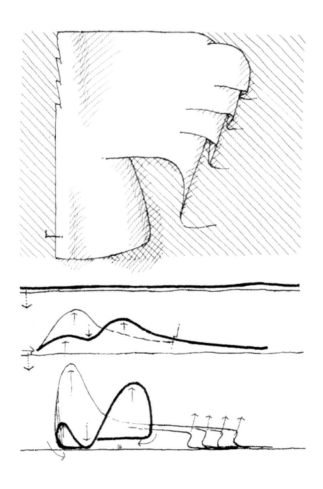

4.27 Heydar Aliyev Center, Baku, Azerbaijan

4.28 Lou Ruvo Center for Brain Health, Las Vegas

rough maquettes or small models of materials that are adjusted, taped together, cut and pasted in search of the ah-ha moment: to be sure, a fine and time-honored method. One can readily see evidence thereof in this project in particular. Here the client group's mandate for something really eye-catching led the large event space which foregrounds the clinic itself to go notably beyond previous such bold compositions of fenestrated walls and volumes: to let them bend, twist and collapse on each other. The unnerving image of floors of rooms thus imploded could be made to happen because there are no floors; all the openings overlook the single bizarre interior of the event space. One might well guess something like an earthquake was the conceptual "cause" but for the waved and torqued once-planar elements: they just got way too overheated. That this is a brain health center causes this image of mind-bending "impossible destruction" to seem an odd choice, but the client is happy: they're getting attention, and it's renting out well for bar mitzvahs and weddings.

Some Exemplars

Having been pretty critical of some works by ZHA, it seems only fair to offer some positive comments. "Landscape Formation One" in Weil am Rhein, Germany is both graceful and dynamic, its composition of linear elements blending with the landscape (Fig. 4.29). This early work is defined by edges as well as continuous curvatures, and epitomizes an architectural experience as movement. With its tiny interiors the project is as much sculpture as architecture, but nonetheless it offers a lesson in the desirability of "smoothing" if leavened by bold form definition, and integration with the landscape leavened by linear expressiveness.

Turning from one of Hadid's smallest and earliest designs to one of her last and largest, the Leeza SOHO Tower in Beijing also partially redeems, in its own very different way, some of the problematic issues of "smoothing" (Fig. 4.30). On the exterior, the gentle and consistent curvatures of the building profile and the glazed atrium gaps don't resort to eroding, stretching, melting, etc., but retain a refreshing almost-dignity. The full-height atrium is another matter, a tour de force of flamboyance barely suggested by the oh-so-slightly ominous S-curves of the atrium glazing-gaps on the exterior. As with all many-stories-high atria, the occupant or visitor is a mere ant therein, but in this case the constantly evolving convexities and concavities of the atrium's opposed interior faces lend a welcome aspect of variety, albeit with a whiff of an inadvertent sense of residing within a whale's ribcage.

Thoughts and issues

All well and good (or more to the point, all well and odd), so what's the point of this litany of 21st century projects under the rubric of "smoothing"? (We'll except the Coop Himmelb(l)au works from the following, given their place as mediators in the narrative.) Well, it seems fair to say that they all, without exception, feature not much of any sense of "anchorage," my oft occurring term for formative aspects visibly linking them to their sites and contexts. A defense of this condition might well be in the justifiability of a clean break, a brave new world leaving the endless boxiness of architecture past in the dust where it belongs. That surely seems to be the tenor of "parametricism," meaning, as best as one can determine without putting too fine a point on it, the application of powerful software to permit a high degree of incremental and mutual adjustment among a structure's parts and parameters. In the case of many of the above projects, this has facilitated a built world without straight lines or edges. But do the means justify these ends? A skeptical postulate might hold that they make them possible—they allow the documentation and thereby the construction of these complex curvatures (and complex they are; one shouldn't fail to note that these projects are amazing achievements of visualization and craft)—but that this doesn't necessarily make them very good: they have opened a pandora's box brimming with a particular sci-fi-ish aesthetic that is often disorienting and lacking a sense of stability or focus.

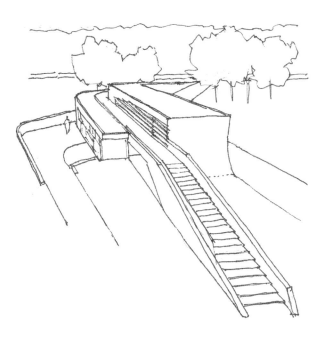

4.29 Landscape Formation One (Landesgartenschau), Weil am Rhein, Germany

4.30 Leeza SOHO Tower, Beijing

PART TWO

ODD INS AND OUTS

Having reached the tag-end of our look at the peculiarities of 21st century architecture, here's a momentary look back at their sequential nature:

- With **obscuration**, morphology is unchanged.

- Three-dimensional stratagems that have some ties to earlier periods involve the breaking-up (or down) into component parts by **fragmentation**.

- Morphological change *without* fragmentation defines the more distinctively 21st century pushing, pulling and twisting (sounds like a kindergarten fight, put that way) of **deformation**.

- Morphological change without *either* fragmentation or deformation defines the reductive, subtractive approaches of **degradation**.

With that brief over(re)view, onward to some peculiarities of its **contents** and **context**.

THE CONTENTS:
ODDITIES INSIDE

Needless to say, architecture is about a lot more than shape and surface, even though that's just what many of these problematic works *do* appear focus on, rather to a fault. If we open the front door (it will often be either shamefully grandiose or a hard-to-find mousehole) and peek inside, a wide spectrum of troublesome "inside issues" are to be found, some of which go hand-in-glove with the oddities of form that have been discussed heretofore. But they also range over the whole speckled spectrum of built form, good, bad and indifferent, of recent decades.

Spatial Matters

Herewith a theory about great big rooms in the middle of buildings (often and oddly called atriums. An atrium is an open-roofed entrance hall or central court in an ancient Roman house: I knew that from architectural history, and Google says so, so it must be right). Anyway, my theory is that at least some of it is about economics. Putting a big room in the middle permits some overlooking spaces to pretend, inadequately, that they can see outside; they permit a building footprint to be big and fat and thereby less expensive in terms of exterior walls and, oftentimes, site area; and they reduce or obviate the need to relate to the outside world. They may have pleasant shrubbery and may have some wide-open use areas that are less expensive to build that self-respecting rooms, and, true, well-crafted "atria" have some environmental benefits, no question. But some can seem empty and alienating: they often lack human scale, sort of by definition, and occupants can tend to feel a bit lost in them. Proportion can be, though not always, problematical, some being too vast to offer a sense of place and some so tall as to be more in the nature of a lightwell (Fig. 5.1). Yes, there are some nice ones out there, but often enough they are a solution in search of a problem: a "statement" wherein a

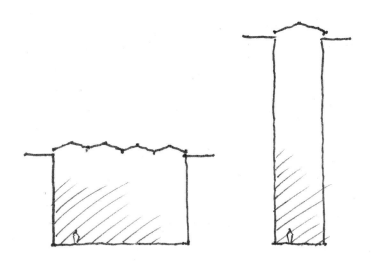

5.1 Lost in the Atrium

like spaces stuffed with presentations going on cheek by jowl amidst the dusty detritus of "creative chaos," an improvement over the old-fashioned rooms? The "jury room" exercises in gratuitous, often downright sadistic verbal abuse on the part of tenured critics have, one gathers, become a bit more civil nowadays, but it seems as if, in many cases, also gone is the dignified exercise of taking your work to a nice space appropriate to that effort of instructive closure, as opposed to a gray corner of a big basement or something much like it.

The Workspace

The design studio matter leads directly into the more general issue of the commercial workspace. In fact, some of the same critique applies, concerning large open spaces paved with long tables, operators of laptop computers lined up double loaded. (Who knows, the pandemic may have changed some of these workspace issues completely in the long term, but the future remains, as always, almost impossible to predict.) Anyway, surely it was unnerving to be constantly avoiding eye contact with the other person across the table; I suppose you can get little baffles for this. That condition appears to have been the new normal—at least before this new, new normal came along—at widely publicized tech company workplaces, even as one suspects that the typical condition at local office suites of regular business sorts remains the cubicle. (And how many Partners, despite the coastal egalitarian notion of moving inboard beside the elevator core so the help can see out, do we suppose have given up their perimeter offices?)

Disliked by many, the cubicle was the brilliant innovation that allowed office

question was not necessarily asked; an ego trip for a designer or a developer or both.

Speaking of big empty spaces that you can feel lost in, here's a sort of a sidebar about another variety of often large and amorphous interior space: the design school studio. To this day, great big noisy rooms full of a lot of design students beavering away appear to remain the go-to way to accommodate "studio courses." The grueling centerpiece of the architecture curriculum, these consume far and away the most student time in the pursuit of learning how to design, even though not so many will spend a lot of time on that activity in their future careers. This jeremiad has its roots in my own long-ago experience with studio rooms— with doors!— meant to accommodate 20 or so students. A sense of place prevailed, as well as a sense of community. Is it the same in the big barn studios, and I just never had the experience in order to know that? Is the cult of ultimate flexibility, resulting in cheap movable partitions that afford no acoustic separation, and corridor-partitions to be depreciated like furniture, not to mention to reduce that expensive square footage consumed by mid-level personnel. It's all part of the great sucking in, the black hole of office dehumanization, increasing "efficiency" for the buyers' and sellers' benefits, a trend accelerated by the advent of the illusion of being able to do much of your work in the space required by a chair and a laptop. The cubicle, much maligned, at least provides a sense of place for an individual, and can accommodate small personal possessions, poignantly serving as reminders that one is not quite the cog in a machine that may often seem the case. Evidently the cog image is the wrong attitude, anyway; we are collaborators, happy to be thrown together in the mosh pit to facilitate a maximum of productive interaction. Evolved trends have eliminated the wasted square feet that personal space required, and the most progressive among us are expected to be happy with the freedom to just perch anywhere—no more bad old regimentation. "Phone booths" and conference rooms ostensibly restore the desirable variety of spatial and acoustic needs, and there's always the pantry or ping-pong or foosball. Why, you would hardly need to leave at all: perhaps next will come the bunk cubicle, if in fact it is not already here: roll in for a while and swing down the hatch for some healthful sensory deprivation. I have a sneaking feeling that a very small minority of brick and mortar businesses across our once great land has risen up to provide such homey amenities, beyond the time-honored dingy break room.

The relationship of the workspace to a "larger sense of a sense of place" also merits concern. True, the rows of long tables do often get divided up into shorter rows (and gaily tossed

around if a Gehry Partners vibe inspires you). At least deadly rows of wage slaves converging to the horizon, the mid-century space-planning norm, are a thing of the past. But what of the many high rises we have seen fit to criticize, or, for that matter, the man-in-the-street-in-the-box that is the far more widespread condition? The outdoors outlook for the work-spacer in the high-rise is often the next high-rise over, or perhaps a vertiginous glimpse of the "atrium" provided in lieu of an actual perimeter exposure. Neither offers a sense of orientation, a home base, a position in the immediate surrounding environment: both are more akin to a fully glazed spaceship, which a fair number of high rises resemble, and with about as much contextual connection.

The box beside the parking lot has its own all-too-easy-to-criticize issues in this regard, for its outlook is not only US Route 441 or the next box over, but some fair number of intervening cars. That said, hopelessly old-fashioned touches such as a small courtyard or a modest laneway with indigenous landscaping do crop up occasionally. One can only hope these reminders that our species is grounded in nature rather than bits & bytes will prevail, since visual access to green space and natural light—to say nothing of *direct* access, an ever more distant option—have been amply demonstrated to have a beneficial effect on physical and psychological health. Those images and those facts sum up an insight one hopes at least a few might share: that a window on grade onto a modest and well-proportioned shared courtyard trumps a glimpse of some high-up urban air any day. Too late for some but not all: the whole notion of the city's intrinsic culture-of-congestion nobility *is* being called into question in some radical quarters—

Floors and Ceilings

To judge from published architecture, we have the lingeringly popular "industrial chic" to thank for a lot of oriented strand board, exposed utilities, and concrete. The look may have come about from several directions: the widespread adaptive re-use of old abandoned factories and warehouses (an excellent pursuit on the face of it); a reaction to the bland corporate look that dominated office suites for so long; and a wish on the part of sleek techies to play house as if in a nobly scruffy startup existence in such "quickly thrown together" stage-set digs.

Regarding the adaptive use condition, whence comes its desirability? Well, beyond the big one of affordability, a variety of textures and materials, along with a variety of interior spatial proportions, have understandable appeal. But the retrofit of the shiny spiral ductwork must be carefully specified, laid out and installed or it will look slipshod, and the random stitching of EMT conduit across those exposed slabs and down those old brick walls has a debasing effect. Said brick is often what was exposed when the old plaster fell down, and a lamentably common practice is to leave the ragged-edged bits of what's left in place, as if this grim "found object" condition was artistic. (Or as if we were too earnestly busy with all that coding to bother. It's simply easier not to try to pry it off, so let's all just agree to pretend that we like the look of living in an old basement, the look we got accustomed to in studio courses.)

As for floors, our choice often seems to come down to exposing the concrete slab or putting down carpet tile of a pattern that fits well with that old basement quality. That is, it often seems to range from black to gray, in a variety of patterns that appear to have had "scuffed" as an intended imagery, and is meant to be laid in an interrupted non-pattern. A final note as to concrete, whether exposed on floors, walls or ceilings: in addition to its unfortunate environmental issues, concrete is an intrinsically unattractive material, really: generally a depressing medium gray and prone by its nature to getting dirty. With the utmost in painstaking effort, concrete walls can be cast and polished into a seductive surface resembling stone, but this is seldom in the cards. As for concrete floors, staining is a popular treatment, if you don't mind the resulting impression that it has been through a disastrous flood and some long-delayed cleaning up has never occured. They do look a little better if polished, exposing the aggregate to varying degrees, but this is a poor-man's terrazzo; real terrazzo is, let's face it, much to be preferred, if it can be afforded, for all too often it all comes down to money.

Ceilings, in many cases in our brave new world, are actually not there: perhaps *the* signature feature of industrial chic is the exposure to view of ducts, conduits, plumbing, beams and corrugated deck (Fig. 5.2). This chaos would be bad enough, but oftentimes steel members must be fireproofed, and since intumescent paint is costly, this consists of that spray-on material that looks like gray oatmeal except a lot bumpier. To say that this is not a good look is to deal in massive understatement. An interesting co-development of ceilings sans underwear has been the incremental *reappearance* of the ceiling, that is, of planar acoustic ceiling panels suspended below all that naked stuff, if for no other reason than that proper acoustic treatment is really, really important. Try to be heard in most any restaurant or nightspot that opened its doors in this century and you know what I mean. A particularly notable aspect of this trend is that these "clouds" appear to be gradually coalescing, leaving less and less of the sans-ceiling guts open to view. It is, after all, the case that the exposed stuff should receive a bit more effort at being laid out in an orderly way than otherwise (a big order, orderly); that it should surely, in a reasonably civilized scenario, be painted; and that the suspended acoustic elements will need some sort of presentable edge trim, these being among the added costs of being fashionably unfinished.

Chairs and Tables

Since all this is about some of the peculiarities of recent modernism, we shall blithely toss aside any examination of furnishings from premodern times. The pertinent point, hardly enough to make a self-respecting paragraph, is that the good work has been done already. Eames, Aalto, Mies, Jacobsen, Gray, Wegner, Thonet, Saarinen, Breuer, that Jeanneret-Gris fellow, etcetera: you get the idea. We are in an age of trying to come up with the next big thing, möbel wise, and in order to be sufficiently original, a lot of peculiar, oddly tweaked items are on offer for today's interiors. And that is because the good stuff has been done already. Sort of tragic, really. (Well, with a few exceptions, one must admit: an Aeron Chair here, a particularly cool tape dispenser there, plus it's undeniably true that there are some versatile new materials and methods available nowadays.) Otherwise what we see is a sea of knockoffs. To be clear, there are *actual* pretty accurate-looking knockoffs, which permit some of us to have furniture that looks really good while feeling kind of ashamed about it, and there are "knockoffs" in the sense that they may vaguely resemble one or another of those classics, but are necessarily different

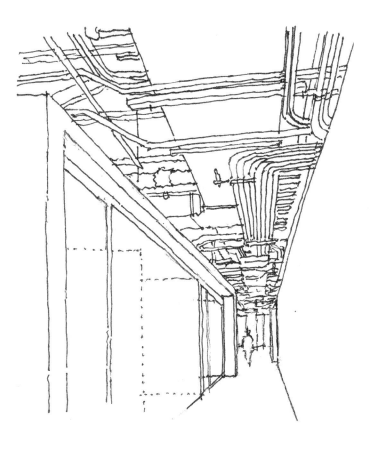

5.2 Ducts, Conduits, Plumbing, Beams and Corrugated Deck

somehow, and since the good stuff has been done already, are just not really as good. I'm sorry.

Having worked our way down from big atria to little accessories, the subject of what's questionably peculiar inside of today's questionably peculiar buildings has run its course, and it's time to go back outside.

97

THE CONTEXT: ODDITIES OUTSIDE

Respect for the context of an architectural project—both the immediate vicinity and the larger cultural vicinity—has long been a watchword of design well done. Having peeked inside selected odd buildings and building trends of the current century, it is incumbent upon us to look around outside as well to see whether that watchword is still in evidence, or not so much: to see whether the peculiarity of these recent years has had a tendency to leak out.

The Outside: Who Needs It?

Some of the projects we have had a look at are sewn up tight as a drum, spaceships indeed, turning their backs on their sites and surroundings. To note a precedent of sorts, some time ago it became a moral stance to be mightily critical of the Portman hotels (such as the Marquis, noted previously) with their largely solid-walled plinth bases turning a blank, cold, streetwall shoulder to the life of the city, their whole rationale being to encapsulate the glitzy atriumized wonders within for the semi-private delectation of their patrons. And yet, so many of the projects we have discussed, buildings in our presumably more enlightened times (along with innumerable others of an atriumized bent), do much the same, persisting in turning something of a blind eye to the world around them. True, that world is often very unappealing, but that's not necessarily a sufficient excuse to ignore it.

It's only fair to provide a specific example or two. We've perused the facades of 41 Cooper Square in NYC, but buried within is a wholly different oddity, a whirling biomorph of negative space eroding its way upward, all about stairsteps and staircases, an Escherish ode to vertical circulation. (This variant of atrium as biomorphic cavern is a thing, it seems, cropping up also in Holl's Simmons Hall at

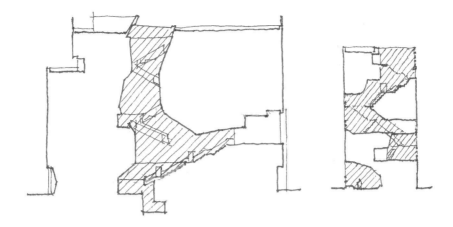

MIT and other interiors of rumen-reticulum-omasum character) (Fig. 6.1). This atrium's one exterior exposure is one of the "torn-open" breaches in the façade, facing a nice view of lushly wooded Cooper Triangle, but it is off to the side, as well as screened off by an awkward pseudo enclosure of swooping grids. So lip service is given to the outlook, but the project really wants to turn inward, it's ripped wrapper all but dissing the adjoining neighborhood.

In contrast, ZHA's Leeza SOHO Tower, albeit of a very different scale and proportion, opens up its own version of a biomorphic interior void with considerable exterior glazing. As with 41 Cooper Square, the atrium is not particularly meant to be a place for people to spend much time in, even if they wanted to. It does connect visually with the building's context, though it's true enough that there's not much of note to respond to in the building's neighborhood of miscellaneous towers, freeways and undeveloped wasteland. The site itself finds the tower isolated, smack in the middle of an amorphous open space otherwise randomly scattered with a few small low-rise support structures. (Fig. 6.2). It sits a bit primly on the dwarfed pavements and landscaping, as if on display on a coffee table like the tasteful vase it resembles. And is that glimmer around its base a shallow moat? These several factors are expressive of a rather aloof disconnect of the building from site and context factors, somewhat contradicting the transparency of the atrium in terms of making some sort of civic connection.

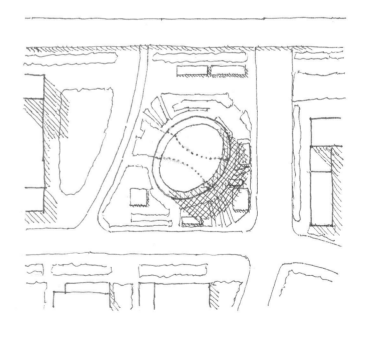

The Art of Exterior Spacemaking: Forgotten?

The Leeza SOHO's treatment of its site's exteriors as somewhat vestigial is a lead-in for the pretty big general subject of buildings' responses to immediate context, and how this has and hasn't been done well in recent years. We've had a look at the Cornell Tech buildings (the Bloomberg and Tata Centers): what of future placemaking as that campus expands south? Well, its award-winning master plan lines up chunky definers for future buildings, the remaining open space largely appearing as just that: remainders, leftovers (Fig. 6.3). One almost expects the main pedestrian way to loop around and end in a cul-de-sac, given a certain resemblance on the part of the plan to suburban developments of chunky houses with leftover space remaining. But the compelling longitudinal shape of the available site forced a grudging sort of main axis to appear, and with minimal notable effort at defining focal points, termini, or a sequence of well-defined and linked open spaces. It's all sort of slushy, mushy, and overstuffed, a bit like the first buildings and, more than likely, those to come.

Another big deal in Manhattan, heretofore of note for some semi-tilting elements, is Hudson Yards. Its high-rise buildings (and they are all high-rise buildings, excepting the merely mid-rise one-percenter mall) strive manfully to look different, despite all having about the same proportions and more or less the same flattish semi-reflective cladding. Since they are mostly basically square, which it is hard for a very tall building to not be, particularly when it is expected to be profitably leasable, they do a right poor job of defining exterior space (Fig. 6.4). Early versions of the master plan showed an amorphous, windswept plaza with any serious effort at making it identifiable as a place yet to be devised; later versions and, yes, the reality, gives us that very windswept plaza—yes, with valiant attempts at "enhancement"— but now with "Vessel" rearing up, a bulbous chess king shouldering up suggestively alongside the queen—the "Shed"— who appears to have hastily thrown on a flimsy nightgown, the two succeeding in stealing each other's thunder (Fig. 6.5). (Please excuse a third chess-piece metaphor *and* the second involving chess-piece nightwear.) Well, Shed at least has a useful purpose, on occasion, whereas Vessel

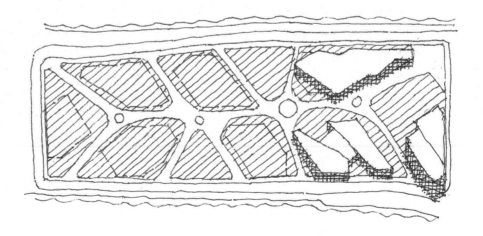

6.3 Cornell Tech, NYC: Site/Master Plan (Showing Buildings as of 2020)

is just a dumb, super-expensive construction, an empty pot serving aptly as the centerpiece of an empty place. It sits precisely where it can also fail to help define axial sequences or peripheral space definition. Sadly there is none of the latter anyway, for the towers rise straight up from the darkling plain, leaving swaths of stone pavement leading nowhere in particular, or so it seems. Two miles away, Rockefeller Center remains the foremost exemplar in Manhattan of high-density-development-urban-spacemaking, its lessons successively overlooked at Lincoln Center, the World Trade Center, and now Hudson Yards.

. . .

Coming back down to something closer to human scale, if that's not too much to ask, one finds that all is not lost: that there are a fair number of projects that feel they must hold the banner of modernism high but still manage to offer more than short shrift to exterior open space definition, wherein the building-as-object gets re-morphed into something a lot more interesting in order to have an interactive relationship with its site context:

- Perkins and Will's University Center at Case Western Reserve achieves something of the opposite of an "object building": its footprint a deferentially residual shape, it has some assertive profiles but can also appear as little more than a very nicely crafted boundary for open spaces that it deftly helps to define, ultimately sloping down gently to disappear at grade (Fig. 6.6).

- In a more compact composition, much of Weiss Manfredi's Vet School expansion at Cornell is connective tissue, linking up big pieces of an existing building complex to configure a spatial sequence, of all things (Fig. 6.7). It

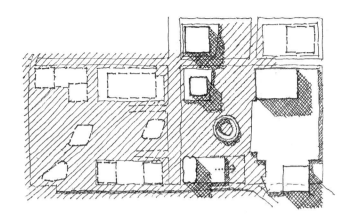

6.4 Hudson Yards, NYC: Site/Master Plan (Showing Buildings as of 2020)

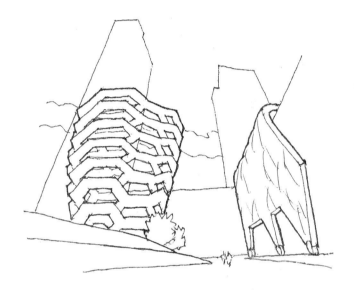

6.5 Vessel Confronts Shed; Overlords Look On

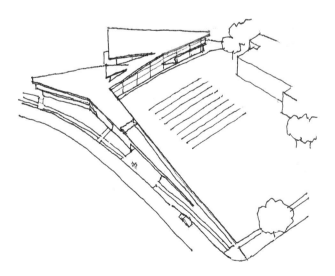

6.6 Tinkham Veale University Center, Case Western Reserve University, Cleveland

101

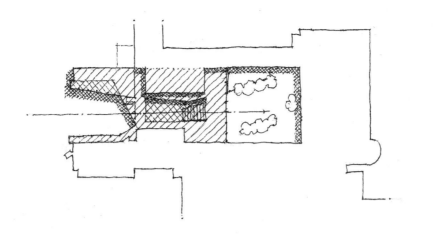

6.7 College of Veterinary Medicine, Cornell University, Ithaca, NY:
Second Floor Plan (Addition Hatched)

focuses to the entrance, continues as a glassy atrium isthmus, and leads on and up to a well-defined quadrangle. The result is reminiscent in its modernist way of some of the closely contained quads of the Ivy League, not to mentioned those of Oxford and Cambridge: still unexcelled and not infrequently overlooked paradigms for campus planning. And the project exemplifies a sensitive and seamless approach to renovation and addition, in contrast to those in the next section.

- Tightening the relationship even further, John Ronan's Innovation Center at IIT brings the exterior into the middle of the building (Fig. 6.8). It's not a simple courtyard scheme, though, but a somewhat complex treatment whereby each of two courtyards connect both to the campus on the lower level and to each other on the upper level. They bring natural light and nature into the building's deep footprint, and without bifurcating the interiors on either level. So although not that apparent on approach, the building's interiors have a truly synergistic relationship with its exteriors, and all but supplant the oft-perceived need for an atrium as a focus.

Additions: Oft Misbegotten?

Additions to buildings are a major aspect of the immediate context of buildings that get them, and a very tricky one to judge by almost any addition one cares to peruse. By way of a special case at the outset, the making of significant additions to "pre-modern" buildings seems often to have been a particularly difficult problem, due to an evident compulsion in the era of modernism to all but ignore the aesthetic scheme of the existing in order in order to

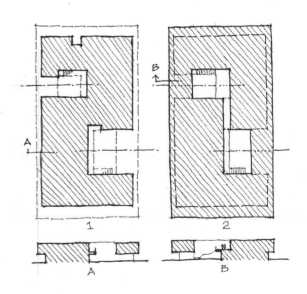

6.8 Ed Kaplan Family Institute for Innovation and
Tech Entrepreneurship, IIT, Chicago

assert the "originality" of the new. The less extreme and more sensible-sounding stance of historic preservationists would have it that an addition to a historic building should be compatible with it, but also distinguishable enough so as not to offer a false impression of being historic as well. This fine line can be hard to draw and is generally colored by today's widespread taboo *against* historicism. (Apparently a long-accepted distinction that "historic" refers to "Washington slept here" sorts of structures, while "historical" refers to, well, old stuff in general, has changed: both are now historic, in sync with our ongoing trend of linguistic simplistication.) Anyway, were the pro-modernism taboo lifted, an addition could be made to a historicist building, without interfering with its proportions or integrity of details, while employing a compatible historicist design vocabulary. And there are some cases where it is perfectly defensible to maintain the very same design vocabulary, as at, for one example, the US Capitol.

Consider the above a sidebar in the defense both of historicism in architecture when merited, and of historicism in additions thereto. But our current building stock under discussion is overwhelmingly—well, entirely—modernist, and some are additions, either to earlier modernist buildings or to earlier-yet historicist buildings. We recall the Libeskind tilting/colliding museum additions: truly exemplars for a foundational debate between the merits of respecting the original or contrasting with it. Both cases are defensible, within limits, although those projects, one proposes, exceed those limits to the degree that they virtually thumb their noses at the originals. True, the originals may be lacking in architectural interest, and deserve

6.9 Addition to Daniels Building, University of Toronto

something done to reinvigorate them, but, really now. A less blatant but no less pertinent case we may recall is that of the frontal addition to the Juilliard School at Lincoln Center, to which the nose-thumbing appellation, as noted earlier, equally applies.

Unlimited examples prevail that demonstrate the evident difficulties such cases present (perhaps, in some few cases, evidences of ineptitude or ignorance as well) in the present century. A few will suffice to make the point well enough for our purposes:

- *Adding to Neo-Gothic:* NADAAA's addition to the University of Toronto's Neo-Gothic Daniels Building—one admits, not the most graceful example of the genre—does all it can to disdain it, with jammed-up junctions and collisions on the part of the assertively modern addition. Peculiar slopes and angles strike no balance with the steep roof forms of the original building but all but demean them, rendering the "difficult whole" less than the sum of its parts (Fig. 6.9).

- *Adding to Art Deco:* In an addition/renovation comprising the Berkeley Art Museum and Pacific Film Archive, DS+R cut some welcome windows in a blank and vacated printing plant, but then appears to have casually thrown a shiny quilt over one end of the handsome front building and called it a day. Some interiors may be inventive, but the deliberate collision of genres that celebrate awkward corners, slipping-sideways junctions, and oddly warped transitions seems a bit of a self-defeating act that renders both the old and new less convincing (Fig. 6.10).

- *Adding to Brutalist:* Gwathmey Siegel's addition to Yale's Art and Architecture Building (now Rudolph Hall) was no doubt a difficult problem, with Paul Rudolph's flamboyant three-dimensional house of cards apparently needing an addition almost as big. Something a bit recessive and respectful of the materials and massing of the original would have seemed achievable and appropriate, but instead, wholly different materials, massing, and finishes shoulder up against it, the new primary elevation now fraternal Siamese twins that do no particular favors for either the old or the new (Fig. 6.11).

6.10 Addition to Berkeley Art Museum and Pacific Film Archive, Berkeley, CA

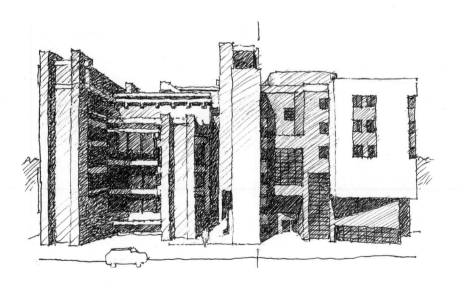

6.11 Addition to Rudolph Hall, Yale University, New Haven, CT (Addition to Right)

- *Adding to Postmodernist:* Pittsburgh's Carnegie Mellon University had a nice run architecturally, initially in the work of Henry Hornbostel and, later, of Michael Dennis. Then the 21st Century arrived and this mutual respect aesthetic (which came with a focus on the old-fashioned and admirable practice of carefully defining sequences of campus open space) evidently seemed so—old fashioned. Despite lip service critique given to the sensitivity of Cannon's addition to the student center, it just looks like, well, like they really disliked the original and simply couldn't make themselves do a respectful addition. It's perfectly ok modernism, but sort of three times full scale relative to the original, and from a different universe design-wise (Fig. 6.12). (This addition, by the way, comes off as the soul of contextual probity in comparison with more recent devil-may-care works nearby that scale up the now well-established nose-thumbing tradition from building to campus scale.)

It's true that additions are generally difficult, but they're interesting: their challenge is one of ending up with a building that doesn't look added on to, but in fact looks better than it did before. At least that's what I always thought. Guess I need to get with the new program.

The extended context

So having strolled outside our odd buildings, we should size up their urban surroundings. The currently existing nature of this extended context is depressing: it's said that 75% of the build environment is put up without the involvement of architects. And we have that expert opinion as to how much of it, architect-assisted or not, is *merde.* Many, though certainly not all, of our odd buildings are objects—"iconic" buildings, if you will—and as noted above, it appears that it can be hard for them to pay much attention to their context, or to each other. A view of a newish coastal area development in Oslo showcases what can happen: chiseled chess pieces all, each about the same visual mass as the last, each striving to be different than the

6.12 Addition to Jared L. Cohon University Center, Carnegie Mellon University, Pittsburgh
(Addition to Left)

6.13 "Barcode Project" Buildings, Oslo

last, lined up for our delectation, bemusement, or dismay (Fig. 6.13).

For the brave new future, one posted approach has been "parametric urbanism," which basically weaves everything into a constantly swelling and shrinking urban rug, with good little parametric buildings all fitting into their slots. There's something a bit repellent about this image; maybe it's the paradox that everything is woven into background, despite the evident tendency for parametrically assisted buildings to be assertively foregroundish. I'd rather look to the work of Alexander, the "new urbanists," and their ilk: open ended and incomplete, but offering a hopeful direction for humane urbanism. For what it's worth, the foregrounders wouldn't fit very well into that vision of urbanism either.

CONCLUSIONS

We recall once again these headers of architecture's new oddities: Obscuration, Fragmentation, Deformation, Degradation. They do sound pretty negative in tone, and as we have found, more or less rightly so. A boiling down of the many and varied problematic issues collected and discussed under those headers reveals another short list: "uber-issues" of oft-recurring matters of concern:

Disorienting

This quality crops up time and again. Is disorientation something to be wished for? A carnival ride or a recreational drug may have this as an amusing side effect, but in the matter of architecture it seems a mean-spirited attribute to invite onto the scene. An excessive diversity of shapes and relationships readily brings this (normally unintended) result. We're all disoriented enough nowadays, thanks very much, by the slightly troubling disintegration of society and the planet, without built environments that twist and tip for no apparent good reason. The generally good attributes of intrigue and surprise can be enhanced by a soupçon of disorientation, but the cook needs to follow the recipe, i.e., not depart too distantly from the central ideas of the scheme (assuming, in turn, that said central ideas don't turn out

to be poster boys of these uber-concerns). Of course part of the problem is that there are no recipes or cookbooks to speak of, for we still largely disdain evidence, as in evidence-based design, as an important admixture to informed aesthetic judgement.

Disturbing

Not simply a darker synonym of the above, this quality is indeed a more definitively negative one. It's evoked in a good many cases by a sense that things are falling apart, collapsing or falling over: pretty good reasons to feel disturbed. A general comment for these uber-issues is that their degree of objectionableness is just that: a matter of degree. Some architecture is and should be exciting, unusual, attention-getting. These are (when appropriate) positive attributes; the caveat is that they go wrong when taken too far, as it seems they so often are.

Erroneous

Regarding error, just that impression crops up often enough among our examples: it looks like a mistake was make; unfortunate repairs were necessary; or, plainly and simply, a bad call was made and an architectonic feature ended up detracting rather than enhancing. Pieces of siding are an oddly different shade, or a piece of different siding altogether is pasted over, or chips, clips or chunks are missing, as if nibbled off by mega-raccoons.

Attention-Averse

Co-opting some verbiage from behavioral studies, this phrase offers a handy alternative meaning for a phenomenon characterizing a fair number of our suspects: simplification to excess. Advocates of learning from the architecture and urbanism of the past and of non-western cultures complain of a lack of textural richness, not to mention a lack of scale variation, in the ongoing world of modernism generally. While these were and are defining aspects of so-called "minimalism," in the present century we find these insufficiencies have risen up to characterize a lot of the big stuff, whether tilted, twisted, or sanded down: buffed surfaces worshipping at the altar of austere elegance and often finding their prayers for the next best thing unanswered.

Attention-Getting

As noted above, not a bad thing in the right context and with the right motives and skill. Sadly, these qualities seem hard to gather successfully into one effort. This attribute may overhang the others as a sort of meta-bad idea when lacking, again, just the right circumstances. Many projects discussed herein can be rightly tarred with this brush of hubris: the architect, the developer, the owner, whatever combination of those in charge, seem to have felt the heady wish to stick out (or up, or over) like a sore thumb.

And as a final shot across the bow, it seems fair to offer that greed and ignorance should share equal billing with hubris as blameworthy for much of architecture's new strangeness.

· · ·

So, the title redux and fini. But it seems a bit too bad to leave it all with a bitter aftertaste. It's worth recalling that a number of these projects got our attention for having pulled things off well despite adopting some potentially odd formative strategies. And a fair number of others, while showing up here for having resorted to a handy peculiarity, were likewise worthy in other ways. In fact, the large majority of these odd works surely arose out of good intentions, whether the result was ultimately a good idea or, as in a good many cases, not.

GLOSSARY

Architect or architecture firm names are not included, excepting some names and acronyms which may be less well known to the general public, in the unlikely event that any of the general public will be reading this book:

Ai Weiwei: Chinese contemporary artist and activist.

ALA: International architecture firm based in Helsinki.

AECOM: International architecture and engineering firm based in Los Angeles.

Aeron: Somewhat clunky looking but comfortable and versatile office chair by Herman Miller.

Belluschi: Pietro Belluschi, respected and restrained mid-century Italian-American architect.

BIG: Too clever acronym for Bjarke Ingels Group, international architecture firm based in Copenhagen and NYC, notable for a propensity to seize on a "BIG" idea that responds in some way to the site or program.

Birdsmouth: In light framing, a triangular cut affording a bearing for a rafter on the top plate.

Blobism: Also called blobitecture. Coined in the 1990's to describe building designs often   reminiscent of internal organs, more readily designable recently with advances in software.

BOA: Bank of America.

Brise Soleil: Term invented by Le Corbusier for a system of parallel sunshades outboard of a building's façade.

Brobdingnagian: Really, really big: from the imaginary land of Brobdingnag in Johnathan Swift's *Gulliver's Travels.*

Catalano: Eduardo Catalano, mid-century Argentine architect.

Caves of Steel: Influential early sci-fi novel by Isaac Azimov; a movie of the same name.

Columbo, Joe: Mid-century Italian industrial designer.

Contraflexive: Made-up term borrowed from structural engineering, referring to an S shaped curve. A variant is sometimes called a "piano curve."

Corbu: Nickname for Le Corbusier (itself a made-up name), the famed Franco-Swiss architect.

"Dark City": 1998 neo-noir science fiction film.

The Dark Forest: 2008 science fiction novel by Liu Cixin.

Deconstructivism: '80's architectural fad characterized by fragmentation and disharmony, the term borrowed from French philosopher Jacques Derrida's opaque theories of semiotic analysis.

DIALOG: Canadian multidisciplinary design and engineering firm.

DS+R: Diller Scofidio + Renfro, an architecture and design firm based in NYC. Refer to comment about BIG.

EIFS: Exterior Insulation Finishing System. Plastic/cement paint on fiberglass mesh on foamboard that can be broken into with a boxcutter.

Empire State Plaza: Architecturally unfortunate complex of state government buildings in Albany, NY.

FDR Memorial: Memorial designed by architect Louis Kahn at the southern end of Roosevelt Island, NYC.

Finlandia Hall: 70's congress and event center in Helsinki designed by Alvar Aalto.

Firminy: Town in central France, the location of several works by Le Corbusier.

Frit: In this context, a ceramic component applied to glass in one or another of a variety of patterns.

Grande Arche de la Défense: Monumental building designed by Danish architect Johan Otto von Spreckelsen, more hole than building, marking the axis from the Louvre through the district of La Défense in greater Paris.

HKS: International Architecture firm based in Dallas.

IAC: An American holding company.

IIT: Illinois Institute of Technology, its original Chicago building complex having been designed by Ludwig Mies van der Rohe in the '40's and '50's.

Innie: A concave navel. Adopted here to mean a self-contained recess or hole in a building façade.

Jeanneret-Gris: Charles-Édouard Jeanneret-Gris, birth name of Le Corbusier. Brilliant, tireless, obsessive architect whose influence almost single-handedly destroyed a mature approach on the part of the profession to what architecture and urbanism could and should be.

Kiesler: Frederick Kiesler, Austrian-American architect and artist.

Kimbell Art Museum: Admired museum in Fort Worth, TX designed by Louis Kahn.

KPF: Kohn Pedersen Fox, International architecture firm based in NYC. First known for its modernism, then for its neohistoricism, then for its neomodernism, then for—

Late modernism: Well defined in a column by Alexandra Lange: "Late Modernism is a style without theory, practiced by architects who were trying to build their way out of the diminishing returns of Miesian copies."

Le Corbusier: Adopted name of Charles-Édouard Jeanneret-Gris, based on a version of his grandfather's name, Lecorbésier. Its literal translation is said to be "the crow-like one" and he did indeed look a little crow-like.

Mecanoo: Dutch architecture firm noted for idiosyncratic modernism.

Merde: French word for s**t.

Minimalism: Definitions vary but generally refers to simplification and rejection of ornament.

Möbel: German word for furniture.

Morphosis: 1: The mode of development of an organism or one of its parts. 2: Architecture and design firm based in NYC and Los Angeles. Purveyor of bold and aggressive design, sometimes evocative of either imminent collapse or imminent attack.

MVRDV: Unpronounceable acronym of Dutch architecture and urbanism firm based in Rotterdam, noted for big, inventive, cheerful, sometimes bizarre designs.

NADAAA: Pronounceable acronym of architecture and urbanism firm based in Boston, notable in part for use of unusual materials and unusual use of usual materials.

Neo-Formalism (or New Formalism): A vapidly decorative version of modernism of the '50's and '60's.

Neo-Historicism: In this context, the distorted co-option and adaptation of elements from architectural styles of the past, to variegate and basically tart up otherwise more-or-less modernist buildings.

OMA: Office of Metropolitan Architecture, Dutch architecture firm based in Rotterdam. Notable for design of often harsh, grim, big buildings which are sometimes, despite this, pretty cool. Mecanoo, MVRDV, OMA—What is it about those wild and crazy Dutch?

One World Trade Center: The tallest building in NYC, in the redevelopment area once known   as Ground Zero.

Parametricism: A style of architecture that relies on programs, algorithms, and computers to manipulate equations for design purposes. The ever-increasing power of these tools permits, for good or ill, an ever-increasing continuity and smoothness of transition among the surfaces and volumes of architectural designs.

Pareidolia: The tendency to perceive a specific, often meaningful image in a random or ambiguous visual pattern.

Pei firm: Pei Cobb Freed & Partners, the current incarnation of the architecture firm founded by Chinese-American architect I.M. Pei in 1955, based in NYC. Notable for monumental,   geometry-forward designs.

Post-Colonialism: More theorizing, dealing in part with moving beyond architecture's "imperial past" when designing for non-western societies.

Postmodernism: In architecture, a movement in the latter decades of the 20th century which reacted to the austerity and lack of variety in modern architecture. Considered a bit frivolous by some. As with most names of 20th-21st century architectural fads, the term was co-opted from a literary movement, architects wishing thereby to also co-opt a frisson of intellectual distinction.

Post Structuralism: Professor Derrida crops up again, the literary arcanity of this term with which he is associated having little to do with the eponymous architectural fad. Post Structuralism in architecture constituted a reaction to Structuralism (see below) and is said to have led to Deconstructivism. Postmodernism is also said to have led to Deconstructivism. Lots of leading, lots of following.

Pushmi-Pullyu: A fictional animal with two heads, at opposite ends of its body, in Hugh Lofting's *The Story of Doctor Dolittle.*

Rationalism: Pick your era: The "enlightenment rationalism" of Boullée and Ledoux; the assorted early 20th century flavors, primarily Italian, of the movement; or the "neo-rationalism," again primarily Italian, of the '60's. It seems fair to say the work in all those eras tended to be flatly and minimalistically monumental, though by no means without some merit.

Rudolph: Paul Rudolph, influential 20th century American architect noted for his spatially complex designs.

Saarinen/Hardy: The reference is to the Vivian Beaumont Theater at Lincoln Center, originally designed by Eero Saarinen, with sensitive 2012 additions by Hugh Hardy's firm. Hardy was an inventive American architect, his firms known for theater design.

SANAA: Pronounceable acronym of a Tokyo based architecture firm, noted for its sometimes graceful, sometimes peculiar designs.

Schröder House: Small house in Utrecht designed by Gerrit Rietveld, presenting as an obsessive rectilinear assemblage of planes and sticks, some painted in primary colors.

SHoP: Too clever acronym for architecture firm based in NYC, working in a variety of idioms, faceting seeming a favored design resort.

Structuralism: A mid-20th century movement in architecture and urbanism in reaction to the rigid qualities of Rationalism. Ostensibly expressing the overarching elements of culture, its own rigidity was reacted to in turn by Post Structuralism.

Tensegrity: The characteristic of a system of isolated components under compression inside a network of continuous tension, a term coined by architect and inventor R. Buckminster Fuller.

The Dark Crystal: A 1982 film directed by Jim Henson and Frank Oz. It has a cult following.

THX 1138: A dystopian science fiction film of 1971 by a young George Lucas.

TVA: The Tennessee Valley Authority, the nation's largest public utility, chartered in 1933.

Villa Savoye: Considered one of Le Corbusier's masterworks, though not from the owners' standpoint: a house built in Poissy, near Paris, in 1929.

WTC: World Trade Center, the lower Manhattan building complex opened in 1973. After the September 11, 2001 attacks a rebuilt World Trade Center was planned, now well underway towards its hodge-podge completion.

Yamasaki: Minoru Yamasaki, neo-formalist Japanese-American architect of the twin towers of the original World Trade Center.

ZHA: Zaha Hadid Architects, international architecture and design firm noted for strikingly flamboyant, aggressive, stridently curvilinear (when not stridently angular) work, generally for clients with large budgets. Selected works have a measure of poetic, sculptural flair.